Living Water

Living Water

A Wisdom Approach to the Parables of Jesus

Robert P. Vande Kappelle

WIPF & STOCK · Eugene, Oregon

LIVING WATER
A Wisdom Approach to the Parables of Jesus

Copyright © 2022 Robert P. Vande Kappelle. All rights reserved. Except for brief quotations in critical publications or reviews, no part of this book may be reproduced in any manner without prior written permission from the publisher. Write: Permissions, Wipf and Stock Publishers, 199 W. 8th Ave., Suite 3, Eugene, OR 97401.

Wipf & Stock
An Imprint of Wipf and Stock Publishers
199 W. 8th Ave., Suite 3
Eugene, OR 97401

www.wipfandstock.com

PAPERBACK ISBN: 978-1-6667-6241-9
HARDCOVER ISBN: 978-1-6667-6242-6
EBOOK ISBN: 978-1-6667-6243-3

10/21/22

Unless otherwise noted, Bible quotations are from the *New Revised Standard Version of the Bible*, copyright © 1989 by the Division of Christian Education of the National Council of the Churches of Christ in the United States of America. Used by permission.

To Jacob Peter

Like the parables of Jesus
you are intriguing—and full of surprises

Contents

1. Introduction | 1
2. Second Half of Life Spirituality | 13
3. Levels of Consciousness | 27
4. Death and Resurrection of the Self | 38
5. The Nature of Scripture | 52
6. The Nature of Jesus' Teaching | 61
7. God's New Reality | 73
8. Jesus and Jewish Eschatology | 88
9. The First Coming of Christ as Eschatological Event | 102
10. Jesus' Use of Parables | 119
11. Matthew's Parables in Nondual Consciousness | 133
12. Hard Teachings of Jesus | 151

Epilogue | 165
Bibliography | 167
Index | 171

1

Introduction

OVER THE PAST CENTURY, the topic of the parables of Jesus and of parables in general has been one of the most exciting and productive in biblical studies. One of the most important aspects of modern parable study is the awareness that the parables are intended to shock and stimulate us into active exploration of their possible meanings through their—at first sight—unlikely comparisons, amoral plots, and unexpected outcomes. The notion of the parables as example studies illustrating well-established moral behavior and established truths can no longer be sustained. Yet the parables are not simple metaphors, but rather extended narratives in which likeness can only be perceived through the negation of literal meanings by an awareness of the strangeness of the plots. The results of scholarly study regarding the parables are encouraging, for they affirm the parables of Jesus are today often read with new, transformative, groundbreaking insights and results.

In his helpful study *A Guide to the Parables*, John Hargreaves indicates that the parables are not tales about extraordinary individuals but stories about ordinary life to show what our ordinary lives can become. If we read the parables in this way, we see the following hopeful things about our lives:

- The parables describe situations in which change is needed
- It is God who offers change and makes it possible
- It is our choice that makes such change possible

Unlike illustrations in many modern sermons, the parables are not didactic in nature but invitations to decision, not aids to limited understanding but spurs to perception and action. If a parable is to strike home to its hearers, all turns on "the moment of truth," some moment in the story when the hearer, like Simon the Pharisee in the account in Luke 7:36–50, is perplexed by the truth in the narrative—not an abstract or predictable literary truth but a truth about the hearer/reader's own existence activated by the parable, forcing that person to perceive, decide, and respond. Using parables to force his hearers to decision, Jesus was giving them an opportunity to change their entire existence—the opportunity of entering God's kingdom or, as John's gospel puts it, of finding "eternal life." Incidentally, creating such moments of awareness should always be the intention of preaching; as Paul put it in Romans 10:17, "faith comes from what is heard."

Jesus was not the first person to tell parables, and despite his originality and creativity, the forms he used were not new. Parabolic speech is a common human way of speaking. Hence, parables of various types are known in virtually all cultures, appearing in various kinds of literature. While parables were a distinct form of teaching in the biblical period, found in the historical and prophetic books of the Old Testament and known and used in the Jewish rabbinical tradition, in the New Testament they are unique to Jesus, the primary vehicle for his teaching ministry. While Jesus did not create the parabolic method, he honed and mastered it and was unique in developing the narrative parable.

To teach by parables is to teach by story-telling. If Jesus had no other claim to fame, he would rank as one of the supreme masters of the short story. As a teaching instrument, the parable is uniquely effective in that it not so much tells a hearer or listener a truth as it enables hearers and readers to discover that truth or teaching for themselves. Wisdom that is merely imparted is quickly forgotten, but wisdom that is discovered lasts a lifetime. Hence, the great value of the parable is that it does not impose wisdom on a person. Rather, it places people in position to discover truth for themselves. A parable has the power of opening our minds or awareness to new insight, but also of making us aware of truth or wisdom already known, but its relevance not clearly seen or grasped (see Matt 13:52).

As a stimulant to perception and action, parables involve surprise. Think of the parables in the thirteenth chapter of Matthew, where we find a surprising variety of harvests, a surprising answer about what to do regarding weeds, a surprising size of the full-grown mustard plant, and so on. Even without reflecting on individual parables, we find that they hide the truth we need by perpetuating an imaginative search for meaning—a meaning that

Introduction

will surprise us when we discover it for ourselves. Parables hide the truth in order to prompt us to do more than simply "hear with our ears" or "read with our eyes" on a literal level (see Matt 13:12 and Luke 8:18).

In the 1960s, when I was beginning graduate studies in biblical theology, several influential texts appeared that signified new ventures in parabolic interpretation. Moving beyond the pioneering historical-eschatological works of scholars such as C. H. Dodd and Joachim Jeremias are volumes by G. V. Jones, whose study of the parables as art forms called for wider application of parables beyond what is possible with "severely historical" approaches, and Dan O. Via, whose influential work on parables focused on aesthetic-existential approaches.

In the first chapter of his *The Parables*, Via discusses parable and allegory. He rejects the currently influential "one-point" approach to parables as "artificially restrictive."[1] According to Via, in allegory the meanings of the various elements in a parable are determined by an "old story," that is, by an actual older story or traditional mindset, way of thinking, or historical situation. What he proposes is an aesthetic interpretation. Because parables are aesthetic in nature, they are not as time-conditioned as are other biblical texts, meaning that the gap between the first and twenty-first century hearers is smaller than is the case with other kinds of texts.

As Via notes, the parables are genuine works of art, and a failure to deal with this fact leads to the one-point theory of interpretation. As a work of art, a parable does not just point inward but also outward. It has meaning within itself and also beyond itself. Via writes, "If the work [or art] operates properly, it is related to the world sequentially as window, mirror, and window. First it is a set of windows through which we see the familiar world referentially. Then the windows become mirrors reflecting inwardly on each other. In this set of reflecting mirrors the familiar and the hitherto unperceived are organized in a new pattern of connections so that in this pattern there is an implicit or preconceptual existential understanding. Finally, the mirrors become windows again, giving us a new vision of the world."[2]

More than a study of the parables in the gospels, this book examines key parables of Jesus to demonstrate what they teach about the importance of shifting our mindset from an egoic (first half of life) consciousness to a nondual/unitive (second half of life) consciousness. The ego tends to resist

---

1. Via, *Parables*, 3.
2. Via, *Parables*, 84.

vulnerability and change, but the shift in consciousness is essential if we wish to use mindfully the time and spiritual resources we have been given.

Many of us still cling to first half of life attitudes and patterns, including such things as reputation, imagined security, unexamined habits, and self-image. We depend on reservoirs of fear, some large and obvious and some small and subtle, thwarting taking risks in our thoughts and actions and keeping us from entering new spiritual terrain of mystery and the unknown. We have no clue what will happen tomorrow, but the only person who can answer questions posed by the often-painful challenges of spirituality are ourselves. And the shaping of our person into someone with greater wisdom, harmony, and fortitude can begin right now, in this moment.

While each of us approaches scripture with pre-understanding, the goal of reading parables, gospels, and the whole of scripture is that those who hear and see with understanding will acquire new understanding (Matt 25:29; Luke 8:16–18). After all, isn't that why we call the Bible "the Word of God" (see Heb 4:12)?

The Importance of Genre in Bible Study

Whenever you read a book, whether you are aware of it or not, you make certain judgments even before you start reading. If you pick up a romance novel, you expect to read about broken hearts or extramarital affairs, but you certainly do not expect to read an enduring literary work. If you read a book on the Vietnam War or the Iraq War, you expect to read about historical events that led to the conflict or the political maneuverings that brought it to conclusion. You would not expect a tourist guide of places to visit in Saigon or Baghdad. When you make judgments about different types of literature, you are making decisions about the genre of the work. The same holds true for literature. Knowing whether the genre of a work is a novel, a biography, or science fiction is an important step in understanding how to interpret it.

The same holds true for the New Testament books; knowing their genre can dramatically impact interpretation. Some people look at the gospels, for example, and think of them as histories (in the modern sense of the word) or eyewitness accounts of the life of Jesus. However, scholarly research into the gospel writers and their intended audiences shows that they were intended as faith proclamations for communities committed to belief in Jesus as the Christ. Similarly, some people read the book of Revelation

Introduction

and think it will give them a timetable of the events that must take place before the end of the world. However, without a proper understanding of the apocalyptic genre, they will miss the intended message of Revelation. The book is highly symbolic, and while it appears to be about the end time, its real message is pastoral, hopeful, and timely.

People who read the Bible with modern eyes, that is, critically, are struck by its varied contents. In addition to historical literature, legal material, and prophetic collections, the Hebrew Bible contains numerous songs, prayers, compilations of wisdom sayings, and similar compositions. Here we have prose and poetry; expansive narrative and short stories; legal codes embedded in historical reports; hymns and prayers; quoted archival documents; quasi-mythical accounts of things that happened "in the beginning" or in God's heavenly court; collections of proverbs, maxims, aphorisms, and riddles; letters to various groups; and reports of mysterious revelations interpreted by heavenly beings. This variety accounts for some of the richness that generations of readers have found within its pages, but it also causes much of the bewilderment even the most devoted readers often feel. How were so many different kinds of writings brought together into one book? This question preoccupies many modern readers and scholars alike.

The New Testament comprises the twenty-seven books that constitute the second of the two portions into which the Bible is naturally divided. Within the New Testament we may broadly distinguish four main types of composition: gospels, letters, theological history, and apocalypses. The New Testament consists of four gospels about Jesus' life, teachings, death, and resurrection; one book of Acts, which describes the activities of Jesus' disciples during the first thirty years following his death; twenty-one epistles written to Christian churches and communities; and an apocalypse, a revelation or disclosure that describes God's will for the future. These books have exercised an enormous influence over the religious lives of Christians for two thousand years and have made a significant impact on the history of Western civilization.

While we can speak of "gospel" as a distinct genre or category of literature often labeled as "moral-religious biography," each gospel contains a variety of genres as well, including quasi-historical narrative (historical data presented through a theological filter), birth narratives, miracle stories, dialogues, discourses, parables, similitudes, moral and theological narrative, prayers, creedal and liturgical material, and passion narratives.

While *Living Water* is primarily a study of the parables, the intention is to encourage readers to apply parabolic interpretation to their reading and understanding of scripture in general. While some of the biblical literature is didactic and intentional in nature, such as the legal, historical, prophetic, and epistolary books of the Bible, much of scripture is highly poetic, symbolic, and expressive as well. Standard hermeneutical practice requires that the biblical exegete become familiar with scriptural genres, interpreting each passage and book according to its literary genre. Having historical, literary, and hermeneutical context is imperative in Bible study. Nevertheless, it may be argued that the biblical text often transcends the author's intentions or mindset. In particular, parables dramatize existential possibilities through concrete historical and sociological details. Likewise, at its highest level, scripture creates ontological possibilities such as living and thinking progressively and fully. Like King David and Nathan's parable of the ewe lamb in 2 Samuel 12:1–4, many of us grasp the moral and religious elements in parabolic scripture but not the further meaning of their application to ourselves.

From Jesus the Martyr to Jesus our Mentor

According to many Christians, Jesus' death was the purpose of his life on earth and was central to God's plan for humanity. In their view, Jesus knew in advance the details of his death and viewed them as central to his messianic vocation and purpose in life. However, in the judgment of many biblical scholars, this understanding of the life and death of Jesus, often labeled "atonement theology," is not biblical and does not go back to Jesus. Rather, it was formulated in the Middle Ages by Anselm of Canterbury (1033–1109), who defined the doctrine of atonement that became normative in the West: God became man in order to expiate the sin of Adam.

While atonement theology is central to the sin and salvation paradigm, prominently upheld in evangelical preaching and teaching, it erroneously compresses the overarching storyline of the Bible into a conversionist template. It begins with absolute perfection in the Garden of Eden, followed by a Fall into original sin (it is important to note that terms such as "Fall" and "original sin," while essential to this paradigm, are not found in the Bible). As a consequence of the sin of Adam and Eve, all humans find themselves in a state of condemnation. Unable to save themselves (that is, to be restored to proper relationship with God, others, themselves, and nature), they are

Introduction

dependent upon God's grace to provide a way of redemption. Because of God's great love for humanity, God sent Jesus to die in our place. God's gift, however, must be accepted by faith, and those who accept Christ as Savior are assured of eternity in heaven with God. Those who remain unrepentant or in a fallen state—which represents the vast majority of humans according to some versions of this conventional view—face damnation to hell, defined traditionally as banishment from God and eternal torment.

Traditional Christians sometimes modify this story line, but rarely do they question its trajectory as a whole, its morality, or even whether it is truly biblical. If it is biblical, did Abraham hold it, or Moses, or Isaiah, or Jesus? Is it explicitly taught in scripture? Was it held in the first three centuries of Christian history? Surprisingly, the answer to each question is "no."

While the Christian tradition tends to present the doctrine of salvation in terms of the ultimate destiny of the individual, this is not accurate, for as the etymology of the word demonstrates, "salvation" comes from the Latin words *salutas*, meaning "security, safety, or wholeness" and *salvus*, meaning something "whole, intact, or in good working order." In biblical times, as today, a viable religion must keep its social system intact, meaning it has to provide salvation at the social level. The majority of current Christian scholars are convinced that the modern evangelical emphasis on "being saved," which views salvation primarily as an assurance of entrance to heaven, is at best a rather recent emphasis in Christian tradition, going back no earlier than the nineteenth century.

In the Bible the concept of salvation had an essentially this-worldly orientation, meaning that the concept was used to assure believers of security from physical and external threats and to guarantee their place in the coming kingdom of God on earth. The paradigmatic model for salvation is the exodus from bondage in Egypt. The Song of Moses, a hymnic passage about the exodus, proclaims God as the "salvation" of the Israelites (Exod 15:2; see Ps 106:21) because God was instrumental in their deliverance from oppression. They were later saved from various other oppressors, sometimes through a human being sent for that purpose: "The Lord gave Israel a savior, so that they escaped from the hand of the Arameans" (2 Kgs 12:5). During the Babylonian exile, God is said to have prepared Cyrus of Persia to carry divine salvation to the Israelites yet again (Isa 44:28—45:7). Thus the prophet Jeremiah could call God the "hope of Israel, its savior in time of trouble" (Jer 14:8).

Living Water

The doctrine of salvation is complex, and different aspects of the Christian understanding of sin and salvation have been emphasized by theologians, teachers, or by different sects and denominations during different periods of church history or for specific situations. Recent studies of the biblical notion of salvation emphasize the importance of contextualization, meaning that because the Christian gospel always addresses specific situations, the doctrine of salvation should be contextualized in those circumstances. For example, to the oppressed—whether spiritually, economically, or politically—the gospel message is that of liberation; to those burdened by personal guilt, the message is one of forgiveness; to the despondent, the message is one of hope.

Christianity holds that the created order, particularly humanity, has fallen into disorder. Things are not what they were meant to be, and something needs to be done about this. The same God who made the created order must act to reorder it, something God accomplished through the life, death, and resurrection of Jesus Christ. In his widely used text *Christian Theology*, Alistair McGrath provides answers given by Christians throughout their history to the question, "*from* what are we saved?" In each case, the doctrine of sin provides an answer. Each model, in turn, also points to the doctrine of salvation, with its hopeful answers.[3]

From what, then, are we saved? McGrath provides six answers: Christians are saved from (1) their human condition, (2) their guilt, (3) their lack of holiness, (4) their inauthentic human existence (characterized by faith in the transient material world), (5) oppression, and (6) from forces that enslave humanity—such as satanic forces, evil spirits, fear of death, or the power of sin. In summary, the Christian doctrine of salvation deals with the restoration of all things, including humanity, to its proper relationship to God.

Salvation, consequently, represents new possibilities, a new state of being. McGrath provides models of salvation that correspond to the six models of sin. Together, they answer the question, "*for* what are we saved?" Christians are saved for (1) relationship with God, (2) righteousness in the sight of God, (3) personal holiness, (4) authentic human existence, (5) social and political liberation, and (6) spiritual freedom.

The understanding of salvation presented above exhibits a radical this-worldly orientation. The reason is clear: traditional Christians followed their Jewish counterparts in placing their faith into a historical context. The

---

3. McGrath, *Christian Theology*, 339–42.

Introduction

basic conviction of the Greeks was that truth was changeless and hence not tied to events. The earliest Christian creeds, such as the Apostles' Creed, were composed to counter such views, which tended to overspiritualize Jesus and detach Christianity from history.

In the judgment of many scholars, the crucifixion of Jesus was the consequence of his actions and teaching, but not their purpose. Comparing his death with those of Mahatma Gandhi and Martin Luther King Jr., one can appreciate more clearly that these deaths were the consequence of their actions and teachings, but certainly not their intention. Looking back on the crucifixion of Jesus, the early Christian movement sought a providential purpose in this horrific event. At least five interpretations of the cross are found in the New Testament itself:[4]

1. A *sacrificial meaning*: this view emphasizes that "Christ died for our sins" (1 Cor 15:3).

2. A *political meaning*: Jesus was a threat to the Roman authorities, who executed him. The authorities said "no" to Jesus, but God has said "yes" (Acts 2:36).

3. A *cosmic meaning*: temporal rulers, whether Roman rulers or Jewish aristocrats in Judea, are viewed as subject to cosmic "principalities and powers," evil systems of domination built into human institutions. According to language found primarily in letters attributed to Paul (Col 2:15), Jesus' death defeats such cosmic powers.

4. A *psychological meaning*: the death and resurrection of Jesus are seen as the embodiment of the path of spiritual transformation that lies at the center of the Christian life, the path of dying to an old way of being and being raised into a new way of being (Gal 2:19–20).

5. A *spiritual meaning*: the death of Jesus reveals the depth of God's love for us (John 3:16; Rom 5:8).

Biblical scholar Marcus Borg argues that in its first-century setting, the statement that "Jesus is the sacrifice for sin" would not have meant that Jesus' death was part of God's plan for salvation. Rather, it would have been understood as a challenge to the sacrificial system centered in the temple in Jerusalem. According to temple theology, "certain kinds of sins and impurities could be dealt with only through sacrifice in the temple. Temple theology thus claimed an institutional monopoly on the forgiveness of sins;

---

4. Borg, *Heart of Christianity*, 91–95.

and because the forgiveness of sins was a prerequisite for entry into the presence of God, temple theology also claimed an institutional monopoly on access to God."[5] Jewish Christians, using the metaphor of sacrifice, were affirming that forgiveness is not rooted in institutional monopoly but in gracious freedom. It is ironic to realize that the Christian religion began to claim for itself a monopoly on grace and access to God that is undermined by this contextual understanding of the meaning of the cross.

As we have noted, the concept of salvation, fully understood, is essential to biblical theology, but the starting point to this concept is not the death of Jesus, but rather his life. In this respect, we must modify the statement found at the start of this segment; it is not Jesus' death, but rather his life that is central to God's plan for humanity. Jesus came, not to die, but to live, and through his life and teachings to illustrate and illuminate the meaning of human life.

In regarding the life of Jesus, the best place to start is with his teaching, and particularly with his parables, for in them we find portrayed Jesus' essential understanding of the nature of God, of God's purpose for humanity, and of what it means to be human. It is this topic—the nature and meaning of Jesus' parables—then, that provides the focus of this study.

Living Water

Speaking of a parabolic approach to scripture, a good place to begin is the story of Jesus and the Samaritan woman at the well found in John 4:6–15. It is an interesting and powerful encounter. When we listen closely, we discover a mutual boldness. Clearly Jesus sees something in this woman from the start, for him even to begin to address her. And far from being intimidated, she engages with him boldly and honestly.

In order to appreciate the poignancy of this encounter, some background knowledge is necessary. While Samaritans and Jews were both Semitic people, descendants of the original twelve tribes of Israel, they had been at odds with each other for centuries, and Jews normally didn't speak to Samaritans. Certainly Jewish men didn't speak to Samaritan women. However, the most direct route from Galilee to Jerusalem required travelers to cross Samaria. At noon, Jesus draws up to a well in Samaria, and asks a woman drawing water there for a drink of water.

---

5. Borg, *Heart of Christianity.*, 94.

Introduction

At first they talk about literal water (the water in the well that one hauls out with a bucket), but when Jesus speaks of living water, the Samaritan woman catches his meaning and makes the leap right along with him. It is a fascinating exchange. There is a heart-to-heart connection and a heart-to-heart inner seeing. Jesus sees who she is, and the Samaritan woman sees who he is. And in light of that mutual recognition, each empowers the other and moves along to greater self-disclosure until finally Jesus reveals his identity to her. It is an extraordinary moment, for it is the first time in this gospel that Jesus reveals his true identity to anyone. Something he sees in her gives him the confidence to be vulnerable, and something she sees in him gives her the confidence to follow his lead, to go higher and higher and deeper and deeper in herself, knowing far beyond what she could know from ordinary knowledge, knowing in the immediacy of her heart. This quality of awareness is not something that comes from outside the moment. Rather, it emerges in the moment of encounter. It is a transfusion from within ("out of the depths," in the words of Psalm 130:1, or like one's depth calling to another, in the words of Psalm 42:7).

The series of encounters not only in John's gospel but in all of the gospels, particularly through Jesus' healing and teaching ministry, result in raising to life and consciousness, to freedom and fullness, the nascent spirituality of his hearers, not only then but now. In the words of the brilliant writer Bruno Barnhart, longtime prior of the Benedictine Monastery in Big Sur, California, "The knowledge of Jesus Christ is a unitive knowledge; it is the luminosity of my own true and eternal being."[6] In the encounter with the Samaritan woman, Jesus becomes the mirror in which she sees not only the face of God but her own true face. It is this kind of encounter, this face-to-face mirroring in which one's depth calls to another, that we hope to discover in our study of the parables of Jesus.

Living Water is useful for individual or group study. Each chapter concludes with questions suitable for discussion or reflection. As you read this book, consider journaling as a way to learn and understand. As you reflect and write, be honest with your thoughts and hopes, without ignoring your fears. In addition to the questions provided, individuals and group leaders are encouraged to add or substitute their own questions. The point of the reading is not to finish the assigned chapter or task, but rather to maintain momentum, that is, to keep the discussion fresh and vital and therefore open and ongoing. Upon concluding each chapter or session, readers and

---

6. Barnhart, *Second Simplicity*, 49.

participants will profit by asking the question, "What is the primary insight I/we gained from this chapter or session?"

Questions for Discussion and Reflection

Having read chapter 1, answer the following questions, writing your answers in a journal. If you are in a group study, be prepared to share your answers with those in the group.

1. Do you agree with the author's view that the intention of parables is to shock, surprise, and stimulate hearer-readers into new awareness? Explain your answer.

2. Assess the merit of Dan Via's notion that the "one-point" approach to parables is "artificially restrictive."

3. Explain the meaning of Via's view that parables operate sequentially as window, mirror, and window.

4. How important is genre to your reading of the Bible? What difference should genre make in our study of scripture?

5. Explain the meaning and significance of "gospel" as a literary genre.

6. Explain the meaning and significance of "parable" as a literary genre.

7. Discuss and assess the meaning of "atonement theology." Of the various interpretations given regarding the meaning of the cross in the New Testament, which do you find most compelling? Why?

8. In his discussion on salvation, Alistair McGrath posits various answers to the question "From what are we saved"? Which of his answers do you find most valid? Why?

9. In his discussion on salvation, Alistair McGrath posits various answers to the question "For what are we saved"? Which of his answers do you find most valid? Why?

10. After reading this chapter, what did you learn about the meaning and significance of the biblical word "salvation"?

11. After reading this chapter, what did you learn about the meaning and significance of the encounter between Jesus and the Samaritan woman?

12. After reading this chapter, what did you learn about the meaning and significance of the biblical term "living water"?

2

Second Half of Life Spirituality

THIS BOOK ARISES OUT of the need for untrained laity—folks in ordinary (unreligious) careers or ways of life who may or may not have been exposed academically to religious or theological studies—to be more creative in thinking about spirituality by engaging broadly with the biblical tradition.

We begin with a common disclaimer. How often do we hear people say, "I love religion, but I hate theology," or better yet, "I am spiritual, but not really religious." This attitude is widespread and is often based on astute discernment. Religion can be impractical, and theology complicated and boring. But the answer to complicated religion is understandable religion, and the antidote to poor theology is good theology. While we cannot speak of spirituality without religious language or apart from theological concepts, the answer to impractical religion and complicated theology is not poor religion or no theology, but rather clear theology leading to holistic spirituality.

To understand spirituality, specifically Christian spirituality, we begin by defining it. We need to do so because in the late twentieth century, the word "spirituality" found wide usage yet went undefined, having a vague association with living holistically, contemplatively, fully, and harmoniously with nature, others, and all of life. This latter perspective, that all life has a spiritual aspect, became associated widely with spirituality, and the term was disengaged from theology in general or religion in particular.

Such lack of specificity, however, makes the concept so universal as to lack value. For our purposes, then, I reconnect the term with its root meaning, that is, with Spirit, or as the ancient Hebrews did, with the "wind" or "breath" of God. To be spiritual, then, is to breathe deeply and harmoniously with Reality (Infinity). Spirituality, then, is a Spirit-filled way of living, walking a hopeful, creative, life-filled path. In using the term "path," I distinguish this way of living from a highway, for spirituality must be personal. By necessity, to choose one path is to reject another. Unlike a highway, a path is not goal-oriented, for spirituality implies choice and even mystery. To quote Matthew Fox, spirituality is

> the way itself, and every moment on the way is a holy moment; a sacred seeing takes place there. All who embark on a spiritual path need to be willing to learn and to let go; to know that none of us has all the answers, and yet that none of us is apart from deity.... What is common to all paths that are spiritual is, of course, the Spirit—breath, life, energy. That is why all true paths are essentially one path—because there is only one Spirit, one breath, one life, one energy in the universe. It belongs to none of us and all of us. We all share it. Spirituality does not make us otherworldly; it renders us more fully alive. The path that spirituality takes is a path away from the superficial into the depths; away from the "outer person" into the "inner person"; away from the privatized and individualistic into the deeply communitarian.[1]

In his public lecture "The Seven Spiritual Laws of Success," the prominent Indian-American physician and philosopher Deepak Chopra defines success as "the progressive realization of worthy goals." Humans are goal-seeking organisms. Because worthy goals involve the ability to love and be compassionate, harmful addictive behavior qualifies as unworthy. From this perspective, a requisite quality for goal-seeking is the ability to hear one's inner voice, to be in touch with the Spirit within, one's true self and creative center. Living out of one's core, one's innermost being, Chopra believes, is what humans mean by "spirituality." Spirituality, simply defined, is "Self-awareness." You will notice I capitalize the word "Self," for this is both intentional and essential to a proper understanding of the concept.

Because it is easy to fall into a simplistic or merely humanistic view of spirituality, let me clarify what I mean. When I think of spirituality, I have in mind the account of Jesus healing a victim of blindness in Mark's gospel. According to Mark 8:22–26, when Jesus heals a blind man in the town of Bethsaida, the healing occurs in three stages. First, the man is blind. Next, Jesus lays hands on him, using saliva to anoint the man's eyes. However, the man's vision is blurry and indistinct. Lastly, Jesus again lays hands upon the

---

1. Fox, *Creation Spirituality*, 12.

blind man's eyes, whereupon his sight is fully restored, enabling him to see everything clearly.

The same pattern can be applied to spirituality (its three stages also understood as three distinct types of spirituality):

1. *self-consciousness.* This stage of awareness—the first half of life phase—denotes "self-awareness," a selfish, self-centered, egocentric state. Characterized by allegiance to the ego or False Self, this stage represents deception and spiritual idolatry. In this stage, a false and dream-like state, humans are in the dark, unaware, and self-deceived.

2. *God-consciousness.* This phase, a transitional phase, is still idolatry, or, more accurately, monolatry, for as commonly understood, it represents institutional allegiance, attachment to ethical and man-made religious belief systems. This phase of spirituality, evident historically in salvation-by-effort approaches, can be likened to sleepwalking. In this stage participants are striving to make progress, but they are still in the dark. They are serving external requirements, pleasing an authoritarian deity.

3. *Self-consciousness.* This stage of awareness—the second half of life phase—is entered through realization, by awakening. Those thus connected to their soul or core being are now "in the light," connected finally to their higher power, to pure consciousness. Such awareness—such living and thinking—are gifts of grace. This state of awareness cannot be earned, but, like the biblical pearl of great price, it can be found through diligent search and desire.

These stages represent the journey from darkness to light, illustrated in nature by the three phases of the twenty-four-hour day: night, twilight/dawn, and day.

The Second Journey

A journey into "the second half of life" awaits us all. This "further journey" is not chronological, nor do we magically stumble upon it at midlife or in times of crisis, though these often serve as catalysts. The second journey is largely unknown today, even by people we consider deeply religious, since most individuals and institutions remain stymied in the preoccupations of the first half of life, establishing identity, creating boundary markers, and seeking security. The first half of life task, while essential, is not the full journey. Furthermore, we cannot walk the second journey with first-journey tools. We need a new toolkit.

How can we know we are entering the second half of life? The following road markers are quite reliable: when we

- experience new urges
- sense a new vision
- are ready to let go of old securities
- are ready to risk giving up the patterns of the past for the promise of the future
- are as focused on the "inner" life as on the outer dimension of life

While individuals can describe their experience of the second journey and even serve as mentors, they cannot define or outline the journey for others. This is due both to the uniqueness of the journey and to a subtle factor, known by generations of mystics and spiritual masters but elusive to many of our contemporaries: we do not choose this second journey; rather it chooses us. It finds us by means of our soul, our personal center and true home, the source of our true belonging. The soul comes to our aid through dreams, deep emotion, love, the quiet voice of guidance, synchronicities, revelations, hunches, and visions, and at times through illness, nightmares, and terrors. This identity defines us, aligning us with our powers of nurturing, transforming, and creating, and with our sense of presence and wonder. The soul guides us, preparing the way and declaring us ready for this further journey.

If we haven't acquired conscious knowledge of our soul, we haven't yet learned of its power. To experience this power, which serves as a bridge to the second half of life, we must first get to know more thoroughly the place in life we already inhabit. This place consists of our relationships and roles in both society and nature. We achieve this knowledge and intimacy through the practice of mindfulness, learning to dwell deeply in the present moment.

This talk of the first and second half of life is not new. It is embodied in the scriptures, tales, and experiences of men and women who find themselves on the further journey. We find it, for example, in the anonymous fourteenth-century classic *The Cloud of Unknowing*, with its distinction between active and contemplative spiritualities, interdependent yet distinct, and in the nineteenth-century existentialist philosopher Søren Kierkegaard's distinction between Religiousness A (a natural form of religious life concerned with ethical standards) and Religiousness B (an ethical life lived in relation to God).

In this second half of life, we are less interested in judging or punishing others, or in harboring superiority complexes. By now these things have shown themselves to be useless, ego-based, and counterproductive. Daily life now requires discernment more than kneejerk response toward either the conservative or liberal end of the spectrum. In the second half of life we focus less on commandments and precepts and more on changing our attitude, on forgiving others rather than criticizing or finding fault.

Life is more spacious now, the boundaries of our lives having been enlarged by the addition of new experiences and relationships. This may be what Ken Wilber means when he says "the classic spiritual journey always begins elitist and ends egalitarian." In the second half of life we are less concerned with mastery of independent dance steps and more with just being part of the general dance. Such people have no need to stand out, make defining moves, or be better than others. Life is more participatory than assertive, and there is less need for self-assertion and self-definition. In the second half of life people live in the presence of God. In that reality, the brightness comes from within, a reflection of the divine that is more than adequate.

Those who live in the presence of God no longer have to prove that their ethnicity is superior, their group the best, their religion the only one that God approves, or that their place in society deserves special treatment. They become less preoccupied with amassing goods and services and focus instead on giving back to others a portion of what they have received. Their concern is no longer to have what they love, but rather to love what they have. When we meet such shining people, we know that they are surely the goal of humanity and the delight of God.

The second half of life journey is likened to the postcritical phase of life or a second simplicity. Paul Ricoeur speaks of it as a second naiveté or a second childhood. Whatever we call it, I believe this condition is the very goal of mature adulthood and mature religion. First naiveté (precritical living and thinking) is the earnest and dangerous innocence we sometimes admire in young zealots, but it is also the reason we should not elect them or follow them as leaders. It is probably necessary to be impetuous when we are young, taking risks and eliminating most doubt. In the long run such approaches to life are not wise. Mature wisdom is content to live with mystery, doubt, and "unknowing," and in such living ironically resolves that very mystery to some degree. It takes a great deal of learning to finally "learn ignorance," as so many religious sages discover. As T. S. Eliot puts it in the *Four Quartets*: "We had the experience but missed the meaning." This means, at least in part, that people in the second half of life need not expect to have the same experiences as others; rather, simple meaning now suffices.

This new coherence, a unified field that embraces paradox, is precisely what gradually characterizes a second half of life person. It feels like a return to simplicity after having learned from all the complexity. Finally we understand that "everything belongs," even the sad, absurd, and futile parts. In the second half of life we can devote ourselves to integrating even the painful parts of our life into the now unified field, including people who are different or marginalized. If we can forgive ourselves for being imperfect and falling, we can do it for just about everyone else.

Some people seem to miss the joy and clarity of the first simplicity, perhaps avoiding the interim complexity, and finally losing the great freedom and magnanimity of the second simplicity as well. We need to hold together all of the stages of life, and for some reason it all becomes quite "simple" as we approach our later years. However, to embrace second half of life spirituality, we must first experience a full and healthy first half of life spirituality, for the two are related and progress in that order. The transition is not clear and practically undefinable, although generally speaking, elements of the second journey are present in the first journey, and elements of the first journey continue in the second. Ultimately, it is love and not knowledge that enables us to reach God in this life.

In the sixteenth-century, Teresa of Ávila spoke of finding God, not through our intellect or understanding, but rather through divine grace, which suspends the human intellect, shifting it from understanding toward love. Thus, Teresa writes, "The important thing is not to think much but to love much," an experience she likens to entering one's "interior castle," a sort of inner structure of the soul that one must enter to find God. The result is what she describes as spiritual marriage, the soul's permanent union with God in love. An earlier mystic, Julian of Norwich, agrees that the focus of one's encounter with God is love, describing the meaning of her "showings" or visions thus: "Do you want to see your Lord's meaning? Learn it well: Love was his meaning. Who showed it to you? Love. Why did he show it to you? For love. Hold fast to this and you will learn and understand more and more. But you will never learn or know anything else throughout eternity."

As previously noted, the transformation that brings us to the second half of life is often more about unlearning than learning. Perhaps it is simply a more profound learning. Life is more spacious now, the boundaries of the container having been enlarged by transformative experiences and relationships. For many people, the second half of life is characterized by seven transformational qualities:

1. Less fear and therefore less hostility. Because we have less need to eliminate the negative or fearful from our lives, there is less need to punish other people. Superiority complexes are shown to be useless, ego based, counterproductive, and often entirely wrong.

2. Less combativeness. By the second half of life we learn that most frontal attacks simply add to the amount of evil within. Along with an inflated self-image, they incite retaliation from those we attack.

3. Less need of attention. When "elders" speak, they need few words to make their point. Second simplicity has its own kind of brightness and clarity, but much of it is expressed nonverbally, and only when needed. In the first half of life, we are defined through differentiation; now we look for commonality. We do not need to dwell on the differences between people or exaggerate the problems. Creating dramas is boring.

4. Less assertion. In the second half of life it is good just to be a part of the general dance. We do not have to stand out or be better than others; life is more participatory than assertive, and there is no need for strong or further self-definition.

5. Less self-concern. At this stage we no longer have to prove we are the best, that our ethnicity is superior, our religion the only one accepted by God, or that our role and place in society deserve special treatment.

6. Less dogmaticism. At this stage we are less condemning. We no longer see God as small, punitive, or tribal. Having defended signposts, now we arrive where the signs point. Our growing sense of spaciousness is no longer found mostly "out there" but especially "in here." The inner and the outer become one. In the second journey, we have less final opinions about things and people as we allow them to delight or sadden us. We no longer need to change or adjust other people in order to be happy ourselves. Ironically, we are more than ever before in a

position to change others—but we do not need to—and that makes all the difference. Now we aid and influence others simply by being who we are.

7. Less possessiveness. At this stage we are no longer preoccupied with accumulating additional goods and services; rather, our desire and effort are to pay back to the world some of what we have received. Our concern is not so much to have what we love, but to love what we have—here and now. This is such a monumental change from the first half of life that it is almost the litmus test of whether we are in the second half of life at all.

Such transformation requires six steps: (1) forgiveness (repudiating retaliation or "getting even"); (2) prayer (learning to listen in silence); (3) changing one's attitude ("unlearning"); (4) quiet persuasion (becoming an elder statesman); (5) becoming an agent of change (which starts with actively working for peace); and (6) influencing events (indirectly rather than directly, by modeling the transformative qualities of the second simplicity).

If unlearning is a way to deeper spirituality, the following pathways represent "paradigm shifts," attitudinal transformations, in the journey from the first to the second half of life:

- Impatient to patient
- Fault-finding to greater acceptance
- Pessimistic to optimistic
- Stoical to joyful
- Independent to dependent
- Aloof to affectionate
- Self-centered to other-oriented
- Frugal to generous

Again, these observations do not represent precepts to be followed or new commandments to be obeyed. The second half of life is not about precepts or commandments, for there is only one guideline for the second half of life: to love the Lord your God with your entire mind, heart, soul, and strength, and your neighbor as yourself. The rest is commentary.

The great difference between transformed and nontransformed people is that transformed people live to serve, not to be served. It is a perspective good parents exemplify. Many of the happiest, most generous and focused people are young mothers. Whole people see and create wholeness wherever they go.

Asking my wife Susan, a second-half person, to identify her tasks for the second journey, she responds succinctly yet profoundly:

1. Identifying and affirming my core self
2. Deepening friendships
3. Accepting my death
4. Redefining my belief system

"What about God," I ask? "Where is God in this process?"

"God is in all of these," she replies, agreeing with Paula D'Arcy that God comes to us disguised as our life.

Spirituality is like breathing—breathing deeply. When you breathe in, you are experiencing or replicating first half of life spirituality. When you breathe out, you are experiencing or replicating second half of life spirituality. To further clarify, I invite you to take three deep breaths, focusing on four elements of the breathing process. First, breathe in fully and hold your inhalation for a while, as long as comfortable. Then exhale and hold the exhalation for as long as comfortable. Do this three times at your own pace, paying attention to each nuance of your breath as you inhale, hold, exhale, and hold. Focus particularly on the empty space at the end of your exhalation.

In this moment, you have nothing to do, nothing to accomplish. For a time, you are giving yourself the gift of being fully present, fully alive, and fully expectant. Rest right here, fully in the moment, ready to receive, then ready to give. Welcome to second half of life spirituality! Receive it, embrace it, and rest fully in its risky fragility. This is the meaning of faith. If inhalation represents belief—walking by sight, clarity, affirmation, and certainty—exhalation represents faith—ambiguity, uncertainty, and unknowing. This is second half of life knowing and living, second half of life spirituality.

Spirituality and Theological Unlearning

The perils of theology, this zealous endeavor to convert a liquid into a solid, are not widely acknowledged, yet they must be confronted and supplanted if we are to grow spiritually. If spirituality is more about unlearning than about learning, the first theological dogma we need to unlearn is the doctrine of heaven and hell. We have learned that heaven is where good people—the "saved," namely God's beloved—spend an eternity with God, and that hell is where bad people—often non-Christians and even Christians "unsaved," according to in-group definitions—spend an eternity without God. It is far better to take these terms, as Jesus does in John's gospel, as references to present experiences. The False Self makes religion into an "evacuation plan for the next world," as Brian McLaren puts it, but the True Self knows that heaven is now and that its loss is hell now. In that respect it might be said that religion is for those afraid to go to hell, while spirituality is for those who have been there.

A person who finds his or her True Self has learned how to live in the big picture, as a part of deep time and all of history. Jesus calls this change of frame and venue living in the kingdom of God, and such living necessitates that we let go of our own smaller kingdoms, what psychiatrist Earl Jabay called "the kingdom of self," which people in the first half of life do not want to do. Life in the kingdom of God is both practicing for heaven and living in heaven. When we do not know our True Self, we push all enlightenment into a possible future reward and punishment system, within which hardly anyone wins. When we live in God's kingdom, we envision a more hopeful eternity.

Heaven is the state of union both here and later. As now, so will it be then. No one is in heaven unless he or she wants to be, and all are in heaven when they live interdependently. That is biblical truth. People are in heaven when they "abide in Christ," living in love with one another, making room for fellowship with the divine, and thinking and living inclusively. The larger and more inclusive our house is, the bigger our heaven. Perhaps this is what Jesus meant by there being "many rooms in my Father's house" (John 14:2). If we go to heaven alone, wrapped in our private worthiness and narrow selectivity, it is by definition *not* heaven. The more we exclude, the more hellish and lonely our existence is. How can we enjoy heaven knowing our loved ones are not there, or are being tortured for all eternity? If we accept a punitive notion of God, who eternally punishes and tortures those who do not love him, then we have an absurd universe where most people on earth end up being more loving than God. Why would Jesus' love be unconditional while he was in this world, and suddenly become conditional after his death? How could Jesus ask us to bless, forgive, and heal our enemies, which he clearly did (Matt 5:43–48), unless God is doing it first and always? Be assured, no one is in hell unless that individual chooses final aloneness and separation.

The second theological dogma we need to unlearn is the doctrine of sin and salvation. John 3:16, the most quoted verse in the New Testament, sums up the message of Jesus by reiterating the salvific dimension of Jesus' death, but moves the argument forward with its reference to God's love. This passage indicates that God's love is directed toward "the world," a term generally associated with that part of humanity that is at odds with Jesus and God. In John 3:16–18, called the "gospel in miniature," we learn that Jesus' purpose in coming is not for the purpose of passing judgment, but rather for the purpose of turning people to God. The context makes clear that Jesus is God's gift of love to everyone, though only believers accept the gift.

The reason that Jesus does not come to pass judgment is because people judge themselves by their response to Jesus. This interpretation is seen in the story of the healing of the blind man in John 9, in crucial ways an exposition of 3:16–21. This story is not simply about the restoration of natural sight. Rather, the author uses this healing story to portray the process of spiritual decision-making. Light and darkness are no longer merely concepts, but are embodied by the characters portrayed in the story. In the blind man's journey from physical blindness to spiritual sight, readers are able to watch as someone comes to the light and is given new life. In the Jewish authorities' passage from physical sight to spiritual blindness, readers are able to watch as the religious authorities close themselves to the light and place themselves under judgment. The dramatic structure of this passage intensifies the profound theological irony: the authorities, who position themselves as judges of others, finally bring themselves under judgment as sinners.

The presentation of sin in John 9 is pivotal to the understanding of sin in John, where the self-righteousness of the Pharisees becomes the basis for their judgment as sinners: "If you were blind, you would not have sin. But now that you say, 'We see,' your sin remains" (John 9:41). In its deepest and most illuminating sense, sin in the Bible is defined not by what we do or don't do, but almost exclusively by our relationship to God. In the New Testament, believers are asked to recognize the transformative power of the love of God and to shape their lives accordingly. To reject Jesus is to reject the love of God in Jesus and so to pass from the possibility of salvation to judgment. The blind man's words in John 9:25 offer eloquent testimony to the transforming power of God's grace in the hymn "Amazing Grace": "I once was blind, but now I see."

The third and final theological dogma we need to unlearn concerns the person of Jesus Christ, the doctrine known as christology.[2] For all practical purposes, the dualist mind is not able to accept the orthodox teaching that Jesus is both fully human and fully divine simultaneously. Rationalist thinking splits and divides, with the result that it understands Jesus as *only* divine and understands humans as *only* human, despite all scriptural and mystical affirmation to the contrary. The doctrine of the Incarnation is designed to overcome this divide, but the practical results for individual Christians, as for Christianity, are disastrous.

The application of the "I Am" title to Jesus, central to the Fourth Gospel, so thrilled early Christians that they forgot the continued need to balance this discovery with Jesus' even more strongly proclaimed humanity. In the synoptic gospels, virtually Jesus' only form of self-reference is "son of man," meaning "son of the human one." The prophet Ezekiel uses this same phrase repeatedly with reference to his mortality and humanity. Early Christian theologians knew this, but they favored an obscure passage in Daniel 7:14 as background, a difficult apocalyptic text with symbolic meaning. When Jesus spoke of himself as "son of man," he was emphasizing his humanity.

Our christology influences our anthropology, meaning that our view of Jesus impacts how we view ourselves. Since Christians mostly think of Jesus as having only a divine nature (for that is how they explain Jesus' ability to perform miracles), they miss a major point he made about himself. Because dualist minds are unable to balance humanity and divinity in Jesus, they are unable to put it together concerning themselves. This is a powerful point, with major implications for Christian thinking and living. If our conception of Jesus is limited to his divinity, eliminating the possibility that he is both divine and human, the result is that we think of ourselves as mere humans trying desperately to become "spiritual," and of Jesus as a divine being trying to look human. The Christian truth is quite different: we are already spiritual (we bear God's divine image), and our task is to become more fully human. Jesus models the full integration for us and, in effect, tells us that divinity looks just like him, even though he looks ordinarily human to others.

Such mystery is the ultimate paradox, and each Christian and all humans struggles with it anew, both in themselves and in Jesus. Over time

---

2. This segment on christology is adapted from Rohr, *Naked Now*, 67–79.

Christians are unable to hold this mystery of Jesus intact, with the result that they fail to see, honor, and reconcile the mystery inside themselves and in others. Nondualist thinking allows us to affirm "the infinite mystery of Jesus and the infinite mystery that we are to ourselves. They are finally the same mystery."[3] What Augustine says about God, "If you understand, then it is not God," we can say about Jesus and about ourselves: "If we understand the Mystery, then it is not so."

In a remarkable statement, addressed both to Pharisees and to his disciples—and therefore to outsiders and insiders simultaneously—Jesus states that the kingdom (the Ultimate Reality) is "not here and not there" but rather "within you" (Luke 17:21). What Jesus is saying, in effect, is that God's actions and presence cannot be limited to sacred times or sacred places, as we understand them, for the ultimate sacred reality is within us!

We must never forget that God loves us because God is good, not because we are good. That changes everything.

Questions for Discussion and Reflection

Having read chapter 2, answer the following questions, writing your answers in a journal. If you are in a group study, be prepared to share your answers with those in the group.

1. What positive—or negative—thoughts come to mind when you think about being religious versus being spiritual? Which term best describes your approach to God or to your deeper Self? Explain your answer.

2. In one sentence, define spirituality.

3. What do you hold sacred in your life? How do you find harmony with this power?

4. If you were to create a hierarchy of values, what value would you place at the top? Explain your answer.

5. Explain the difference between "self-consciousness" and "Self-consciousness."

6. Do you consider yourself to be in the first or second half of the spiritual journey? Explain your answer.

3. Rohr, *Naked Now*, 70.

7. Of the eight pathways or "paradigm shifts" listed in this chapter, which attitudinal shift do you find most compelling at this point in your life? Explain your answer.

8. Assess the validity of Paula D'Arcy's assertion that God comes to us disguised as our life.

9. If spirituality involves unlearning, which theological dogma(s) do you need to unlearn? Explain your answer.

10. Do you tend to view God as friend, adviser, therapist, or judge? Explain your answer. In your estimation, how does your view of God affect your self-image? How does your view of God affect how you treat and view others?

11. How does your view of God affect how you understand the doctrines of sin and salvation? Of heaven and hell?

12. How does your view of God affect your christology?

3

Levels of Consciousness

ONE OF THE GREAT thinkers of our time is philosopher Ken Wilber, whose writings identify the existence of numerous levels of consciousness, from prepersonal to personal to transpersonal, beginning with the archaic consciousness of infants and early Stone Age people through the highest stages of nondual consciousness. In the model below, I reduce his stages to five:

- Stage Zero: archaic consciousness. This is the basic state of survival, in which the senses reign and a person is defined by basic needs. Today this is the stage of infants and of aged people suffering from some degenerate disorder.
- Stage One: tribal/familial consciousness. This state, dualist by nature, focuses on the distinction between good and evil. Highly ritualistic and emphasizing kinship ties, Wilber describes it as "exterior individual."
- Stage Two: egoic consciousness. This state, an extension of archaic consciousness, is highly individualistic and consumer oriented. Wilber describes it as "interior individual."
- Stage Three: rational/scientific consciousness. This stage is pragmatic and focuses on achievement and progress. Wilber describes it as "interior collective."
- Stage Four: mystical/unitive consciousness. This stage focuses on community and shared progress. In this stage, described by Wilber as "exterior collective," dogma, greed, and division are extinguished, and

the focus is on harmony between human beings and the potential of human development.

Adhering to Wilber's paradigm, Stage Zero is a prepersonal phase; Stages One through Three represent aspects or dimensions of a personal phase, and Stage Four is a transpersonal phase. In Jesus' time, most people were in Stage One form of consciousness, their sense of identity oriented collectively around membership in a specific tribal, kinship, or sectarian group. Today, the majority of people in the West find themselves ensconced in Stage Two egoic (consumer) mindset, with a Stage Three (rational/scientific) overlay. However, when pushed by fear or uncertainty, the more primitive group (tribal) mentality still reasserts itself. Throughout history, only a small minority attained to Stage Four, a visionary, nondual consciousness still rare in our own time. This is what made Jesus, likely the first nondual sage of his era, such an enigma, not only to his original audience but even to this day, calling people to a radical transformation of consciousness several stages above their understanding and still above our own. No wonder it is difficult to catch the subtlety of his teaching. The Bible, it seems, can be read with a lower level of consciousness, though its higher teaching, such as its parabolic nature, requires a visionary Stage Four level of understanding.

Why is a change or transformation of consciousness from dual to nondual necessary? Because we cannot authentically love another or forgive another's offenses inside of dualistic consciousness. In our habitual, dualistic way of thinking, we view ourselves as separate from God and from each other. The church has done the people of God a great disservice by preaching the gospel to them but not giving them the tools whereby they can obey that gospel. As Jesus put it, "apart from me you can do nothing" (John 15:5). The "vine and branches" is one of the greatest Christian mystical images of the nonduality between God and the human soul. In and with God, we can love and forgive everything and everyone—even our enemies. Alone and by ourselves, we will seldom be able to love in difficult situations over time through our own willpower and intellect.

Nondual consciousness is a new way of Jesus. Spiritual maturity is largely growth in seeing. Full seeing seems to take most of our lifetime. There is a cumulative and exponential growth in perception for those who do their inner work. This is also a cumulative closing down in people who deny shadow work and humiliating self-knowledge. This is the classic closed mind and heart that we see in many adolescents, young adults, and even in some older people. The longer we persist in dualistic living and thinking, the harder it becomes because we have more and more years of illusion to justify. For that reason it is important to allow transformation of consciousness as soon as possible, for it gets harder with time.

All physical shadows are created by a mixture of darkness and light, and this is the only spectrum of human vision. We cannot see inside of total light or total darkness. As the shadows of things gradually manifest themselves as understandable and real, we lose interest in idealizing or idolizing persons or events, especially ourselves. As Jesus said to the rich young man, "No one is good but God alone" (Mark 10:18). All created things are a mixture of good and not so good.

This does not mean we stop loving other people; in fact, it means we actually begin to truly love people and all creatures. It does not mean self-hatred or self-doubt, but finally accepting and fully owning both our gifts and our weaknesses; they no longer cancel one another out. We can eventually do the same for others, and we do not let another's faults destroy our larger relationship with them. This is why nondual thinking is absolutely necessary for human flourishing. It is the change that changes everything else. It makes love, forgiveness, and patience possible. Without it, we are forever trapped inside of our judgments.

In *Holistic Happiness*, I present a model similar to Wilber's, which I label the "five halves of life."[1] Understanding the term "half" symbolically rather than literally, I speak of five dimensions or mindsets that people may acquire through life, including a preparatory stage or "half" (Phase 0) and then two essentially secular/religious halves, which I call first and second half living and thinking (Phases 1A and 1B), themselves mirroring two spiritual phases called first and second half of life spirituality (Phases 2A and 2B), configured as follows:

1. Preparatory Half (Phase 0): preconventional morality (childhood and adolescence)

2. First Half Living and Thinking (Phase 1A): conventional morality (late adolescence through adulthood)

3. Second Half Living and Thinking (Phase 1B): postconventional morality (late adolescence through adulthood)

4. First Half of Life Spirituality (Phase 2A): conventional religiosity (late adolescence through adulthood)

---

1. Vande Kappelle, *Holistic Happiness*, 9–16.

5. Second Half of Life Spirituality (Phase 2B): postconventional spirituality (late adolescence through adulthood)

In Phase 0, individuals are ruled by the senses, concerned primarily with self-gratification, and live for the present. Individuals in this phase (including most children, youth, adolescents, and some adults) may have special and unique spiritual dispositions and experiences, but such experience is immature and unformed. On the whole, their beliefs, behavior, and outlook is best characterized as preparatory or preconventional, since their character and personality, like their morality and brains, is mostly borrowed, imitated, untested, and not yet fully formed. This phase revolves around the mental function of sorting nearly everything into one of two categories (things are either permitted or prohibited, others are either friend or foe, and one is either happy or sad). For that reason, in Phase 0, you set out to master the mental skills of dualism, of seeing the world in twos (this or that, in or out, right or wrong). Phase 0 is the baseline of what being raised means in our culture. Here one is taught the difference between right and wrong and other basic dualisms.

At some point in their socializing growth, youth begin accommodating to those around them, joining peer groups and aspiring to be admired and respected by others. Entering the first half of living and thinking, such individuals are shaping, developing, and testing their identity. Authorities—parents, grandparents, teachers, political and religious leaders—are central to this phase. Phase 1A is the phase of authority as well as of dualism. While some individuals at this point become relatively autonomous, the majority desire to be like their elders, valuing and depending on their authority. They trust authorities and wish to please them, and they aspire to be as certain and all-knowing as they are. As far as they are concerned, the authorities know everything, and they do not, so they feel highly dependent on them. Before long, they find out that the authorities in their life dislike or distrust other authorities, and their dualism adds a new category: us versus them. This social dualism creates a strong sense of loyalty and identity among "us." It also creates a strong sense of anxiety and even hostility about "them," the "others," the "outsiders," and the "outcasts." Phase 1A is built on trust, because at that stage, trust is an absolute necessity, a matter of survival. Simple trust and unquestioning loyalty are what matters in Phase 1A.

While this phase works well with adolescents and young adults, many people spend their entire lives in Phase 1A, submitting to authorities and

Levels of Consciousness

following all the rules. Then, when it is time for them to become authorities themselves, they demand the same submission from the next generation that they themselves gave to the previous generation. For that reason, it shouldn't be a surprise that faith and religion are a strictly Phase 1A phenomenon for millions, even billions, of people.

Thus far, Phase 1A may feel like a school to help people learn the basic morals necessary for independence. However, at some point, this phase becomes confining or restrictive, and individuals begin to question whether authorities are always right. They may even question whether rules are always absolute and appropriate. This may happen at twelve or twenty-two or forty-five, but eventually, many enter Phase 1B. If Phase 1A is about dualism and dependence, Phase 1B is about pragmatism and independence. People in this phase recognize they have their own lives to live, and they have to find a way to become who they are on their own.

In Phase 1A they were drawn to authority figures who told them what to think and do, but in Phase 1B they seek out coaches who teach them how to think for themselves and help them develop their own goals, along with their own skills to attain those goals. In Phase 1A they saw life as a matter of survival, but in Phase 1B they see life as a game, as a contest of competing and winning. In Phase 1A everything was either known or knowable, but in Phase 1B, everything is learnable and doable, if only they can find the right models, mentors, and coaches, and master the right techniques, skills, and know-how.

When people run into problems with Phase 1A living and thinking, some may temporarily or permanently resort to Phase 0 behavior and belief, living solely for pleasure and ego-gratification. However, many Phase 1A individuals abandon dualism and pragmatism, together with authoritarian leaders, dogmatic mindsets, and moralistic standards, and commit instead to global and pluralistic values, loving others selflessly, simplifying lifestyle, living generously and compassionately, committing to social, ecological, political, and economic issues and concerns. Becoming atheists, agnostics, or merely nonbelievers, such individuals only achieve this stage secularly and nonspiritually.

While we are now familiar with the expression "the first and second halves of life," we should not, indeed we cannot equate them with first and second half of life spirituality. While there are similarities and overlap between these formulations, the first expression refers essentially to chronology, distinguishing immaturity from maturity, youth and adulthood from midage and old age, starting life from concluding life.

By contrast, first and second half of life spirituality, while often working in tandem with first and second half of life living and thinking, is a way of life and thought that though religious in nature, is centered on encounter with deity/divine Spirit, with opening to grace as the foundational event. However, for many if not for most individuals, piety, religion, morality, and even culture take the place of spirituality. In such cases, nominal religion becomes religiosity, a substitute for authentic spirituality, and in speaking of religiosity, we find we are no longer describing spirituality but rather an acculturated form of first half of life living and thinking. For many people, particularly those brought up in evangelical Christian homes, Phase 1A (first half living and thinking) and Phase 2A (first half of life spirituality) are experienced concurrently, for they find themselves living dualistically, adapting to secular and religious rules and guidelines simultaneously.

According to our model, it is quite natural for many children brought up in traditional Christian households to bypass Phases 1A and 1B altogether and enter Phase 2A spirituality at an early age. As is true of Phase 1A, Phase 2A, understood as a moral/religious phase common to evangelical Christianity, is centered on acquiring essential religious beliefs and mastering dualistic mental skills such as sorting things into opposing categories such as right or wrong, true or false, sacred or secular, good and evil, and others as friends or foes. Authorities such as parents, teachers, and religious leaders are central to this way of being religious or spiritual.

In my experience and from my vantage point as a scholar of spirituality and religious studies, the entry point to authentic spirituality, unlike much moral and religious belief and behavior, is not ritual or indoctrination, although these can be catalysts for first half of life spirituality, but rather a personal or individual encounter with the divine. This experience, called a "second birth" by evangelicals, profession of faith and baptism by Baptists, speaking in tongues or Spirit-filled living by Pentecostals, confirmation by Catholics, or Bar Mitzvah by Jews, is frequently the foundational experience for first half of life spirituality. Such events are usually euphoric, but such euphoria is often short-lived, for this experience is frequently followed by conformity, rigid religious belief, and moralistic behavior.

Because Phase 2A spirituality is highly dualistic, such dualism is divisive and, like Phase 1A, it creates a strong sense of loyalty and identity. It also creates a strong sense of anxiety and even hostility toward "outsiders," "backsliders," and "outcasts." At some point in the faith journey, Phase 2A believers are no longer content merely to listen to a sermon by an authority figure; they want to learn methods of studying the Bible for themselves. Learning and studying, thinking for themselves and reaching their own conclusions, are part of what it means to be a good Phase 2A believer. Such people become active consumers in the religious market. Every year, they need more sermons, books, radio and TV shows, podcasts, conferences, courses, retreats, camps, churches, and mission trips. For some Phase 2A people, their faith never exceeds the authoritarian, dualistic faith of Phase 2A spirituality, while others never exceed the inquisitive, pragmatic side of dogmatic faith. Others, however, outgrow this phase altogether, questioning their religious goals, needs, and priorities.

When people run into problems with Phase 2A spirituality, some transfer to another faith community. Other disillusioned Phase 2A believers temporarily or permanently revert to phase 1 standards, perspectives, and forms of living. When Phase 2A people find religious teaching or programming doesn't produce the results they expect, many sincere believers simply amp up their effort, assuming the fault is their own. Many modern individuals, however, experience a profound loss of religious confidence, and their Phase 2A spirituality starts to collapse. For most such believers, there is no going back, at least not in the long term. Having felt increasingly alienated from Phase 2A spiritual dualism and theological dogmatism, they lose faith in both authoritarian leaders and success coaches, whether inside or outside the church. Both types of leaders made promises they couldn't deliver, and neither type honestly faced life's deeper questions and challenges.

While some Phase 2A believers start doubting the whole faith project, others aren't so easily satisfied. Their quest for honesty and depth burns like a fire in the belly and they move into Phase 2B spirituality. If such Phase 2A believers remain open and patient, many encounter a moment of crisis, and they find themselves actors in a deeper narrative that embraces and integrates all things, producing a way to see things whole again. This second awakening produces seekers, transformed by what might be called "an experience of sacred mystery." Something has happened to them—a mystical experience, something traumatic, a relationship, a sudden realization, a wilderness experience, an experience of "something more"—and the word "God" became meaningful once again, only this time not as a reference to a supernatural being "out there" but to the sacred at the center of existence, the holy mystery that is all around us and within us. No longer a mere idea or an article of belief external to oneself, God has become an element of experience. Such persons have reached Phase 2B spirituality (also called second naiveté), a state where they participate in religious rituals because they are meaningful and not because they are required, where they hear ancient biblical stories as "true" while knowing them as not literally true.

Looking back, they discover that they still retain powerful and valuable treasures gained in previous phases. Though nondualists, they appreciate the lessons of dualism, which taught them to distinguish right from wrong and good from evil, and to care about their choices. From earlier phases, they also learned to be curious and flexible. They also learned that different phases of life operate by different sets of rules. In addition to becoming independent, self-motivated, and self-managed adults who take responsibility for their own successes and failures, they also learned that doubt and perplexity bring some of the greatest spiritual gifts life has to offer, gifts such as humility, honesty, courage, and sensitivity. Critical of their own critical thinking, skeptical of their own skepticism, they begin to wonder, hope, and imagine, and they dare to believe that there is a better second half of life, a better half of spirituality. To maintain momentum, to keep growing and developing, however, requires a kind of dying, a death to ego or pride, a relinquishment of our right to judge, to know, and to control. You might call this a death to privilege, superiority, or supremacy, as seekers realize that all people share in the human condition.

Phase 2B spirituality builds on "the still more excellent way of love" described by Paul in his letter to the Corinthians (1 Cor 12:31—14:1). In this passage, Paul makes clear that nearly everything religious people strive for will eventually be embraced by something deeper. Even faith and hope don't have the last word. Only love, he says, is the more excellent way. In this phase, we can finally accept that all our knowing, past and present, is partial (1 Cor 13:12). Phase 2B seekers finally see authority figures as mortal and fallible human beings. This awareness also allows them to find their identity in new ways in relation to others; not in Phase 2A dependence on fallible authority figures but in the more mature interdependence of nonduality. This humility before others morphs into the realization that no statement about God—or even about what is true—can be final or complete.

This new realization—likened to a second naiveté, a second simplicity or innocence best described as transcendence, combines the best of the conservative and the best of the progressive positions, because it brings along or includes the previous stages rather than leaving them behind.

Phase 2B spirituality eventually matures into a higher spirituality, continuing in an ascending spiral of growth and discovery that lasts as long as life itself. Far from feeling they have finally arrived, Phase 2B seekers finally begin to understand that arrival has never been the goal. Rather, Phase 2B spirituality allows seekers to discover amazing truths. For example, they discover that spirituality is about love; that knowing is loving; that they know themselves by loving themselves; that they know others by loving them; that they know God by loving themselves and others. Those who reach Phase 2B spirituality do not experience certainty, however, for that is the concern of those in earlier phases. Phase 2B seekers never feel they have arrived. They are not obsessed with misguided notions of certainty or supremacy—more the opposite. Committed to the faith journey, they know there is no such thing as certainty in faith. Faith, like all creativity, flourishes not in certainty but in questioning, not in security but in venturing. In Phase 2B spirituality, it is trust that matters, and qualities such as peace, harmony, joy, relationships, intimacy, and unity.

While some form of awakening (spiritual conversion or "spiritual rebirth") may be foundational for second half of life spirituality, this experience differs from similar first half of life conversion in that for this second "half" of life, such an experience is not based on a decision one makes or a commitment one controls. Rather, this experience is an absolute gift of grace, for it comes more as a realization or revelation than as an act of the will. Unlike entrance into first half of life spirituality, this second experience is best described as a realization or awakening, for such transformation simply happens over time, more like a process than an event, and it may take time before individuals become conscious of the changes within themselves. More commonly, awareness occurs retrospectively, brought to our attention by those around us who notice the difference in our attitude, nature, and demeanor.

According to the five halves of life model, spirituality is not a specific way of living and thinking, nor a way of being moral or religious, but rather is a mature and selfless way of being. While first half of spirituality (Phase 2A) may be initiated by individuals and can look like religious living and thinking, second half of spirituality (Phase 2B) is initiated and led by the Divine Spirit. In both cases, individuals are oriented consciously and unconsciously toward the Divine, understood to be present both immanently and transcendently.

While individuals can describe their own experience of the second spiritual journey and even serve as mentors, they cannot define or outline the journey for others. This is due both to the uniqueness of the journey and to a subtle factor, known by generations of mystics and spiritual masters but elusive to many of our contemporaries: One does not choose this second spiritual journey; rather, it chooses you. It finds you by means of your soul, your personal center and true home, the source of your true belonging. The soul comes to our aid through dreams, deep emotion, love, the quiet voice of guidance, synchronicities, revelations, hunches, and visions, and at times through illness, nightmares, and terrors. This is the identity that defines us, aligning us with our powers of nurturing, transforming, and creating, with our powers of presence and wonder. It is the soul that guides us, preparing the way and declaring us ready for this further journey.

As you may have guessed, the use of the phrase "five halves of life" in this chapter serves as a *koan*, that is, as an irrational riddle designed to stimulate your deepest intuition and to help you remain open to the limitless possibilities associated with spirituality. Viewed literalistically or on an elementary level, there can only be two halves of life, rather than three, four, or five. From this perspective, the five halves of life model is reducible to two halves or dimensions of life, one set of halves for the False Self or ego and one set for the True Self or soul, both preceded by a preparatory or preliminary phase or dimension.[2]

Questions for Discussion and Reflection

Having read chapter 3, answer the following questions, writing your answers in a journal. If you are in a group study, be prepared to share your answers with those in the group.

1. After reading this chapter, what did you learn about levels of consciousness?
2. After reading this chapter, what did you learn about phases of spirituality?
3. Assess the validity of Ken Wilber's five levels of consciousness.

---

2. The distinction between False and True Self is discussed in chapter 4 below.

Levels of Consciousness

4. Do you agree with the author that a change or transformation from dual to nondual forms of consciousness is necessary for spiritual growth and effectiveness? Explain you answer.

5. If nondual consciousness exemplified the mindset of Jesus, can you provide examples from his life and teaching?

6. In your estimation, what was Jesus implying in Mark 10:18 when he told the rich your man, "No one is good but God alone"? By this determination, was Jesus claiming humanity and disavowing deity? Explain your answer.

7. Assess the validity of the model the author calls the "five halves of life," and indicate the phase that best describes your current spiritual state. Explain your answer.

8. Do you agree that there are three distinct phases of morality, which the author labels preconventional, conventional, and postconventional? If so, what are the differences between them?

9. Do you agree that there are two distinct phases of spirituality, which the author labels conventional religiosity (Phase 2A) and postconventional spirituality (Phase 2B)? If so, what are the differences between them?

10. Explain the distinction between second half of life living and thinking (Phase 1B) and second half of life spirituality (Phase 2B).

11. Assess the validity of the author's statement that some form of awakening or spiritual conversion is (or may be) foundational for second half of life spirituality.

12. Explain and assess the meaning of the author's statement, "One does not choose the second journey; rather, it chooses you."

4

Death and Resurrection of the Self

MODERN WESTERN SOCIETY PRESENTS a rosy picture: the journey ahead is upward and onward. You can be successful, and you can do it by yourself. Jesus, however, presents us with a different model, that of death and resurrection—a pattern of renewal, of daily dying to self. This leaves us with an important question, "How much False Self are we willing to shed to find our True Self?" The True Self is who you are from the beginning, in the heart of God, the "face we had before we were born," as the Zen masters say. In this light, Swiss psychiatrist Carl Jung offered a momentous insight: "Life is a luminous pause between two great mysteries, which themselves are one." In his inimitable way, Irish poet William Butler Yates probed deeper when he wrote, "Many times man lives and dies between his two eternities."

Life's ultimate adventure, its grandest game and greatest challenge, is the spiritual transformation (rebirth) of the self. As I discuss in many of my writings on spirituality, the role of authentic spirituality is letting go of the False Self, one's incomplete self trying to pass for one's True Self. Our True Self, our inherent soul, is that part of us that sees reality accurately, truthfully. It is divine breath passing through us, dwelling with us. Our False Self is the egoic self that is limited and constantly changing. It masquerades as true and permanent but in reality is passing, tentative, and fearful of change. It is that part of us that will eventually die. The role of true spirituality, of mature religion, is to help speed up this process of dying to the False Self.

Not surprisingly, we cannot accomplish—or even understand—what we have not been told to look for or to expect. This staggering change of perspective—that our ego is not our True Self—is what Jesus came to convey to humanity. It led Thomas Merton, the Trappist monk who first suggested use of the term False Self, to his radical rediscovery of the meaning of Jesus' teaching that his followers must lose their False Self in order to discover their True Self (see Mark 8:35).

Unfortunately, many traditionalists remain quite rigid in their thinking because they have been taught that faith requires adherence to the religious status quo, and with it unquestioned obedience to the guardians of tradition. Such people are often moral and productive—even model citizens—but they underrate the centrality of paradox or mystery to the faith traditions they espouse. When many religious practitioners observe rituals faithfully without experiencing spiritual transformation at any deep level, religion becomes a duty that actually prevents transformation from taking place. This has been going on for centuries, and in all faith traditions.

Mature religion talks about the death of any notion of a separate, False Self, while recognizing that only a deep security in a larger love will give us the courage to do that. The True Self can let go because it is secure at its core. Our False Self, however, does not let go easily. As Jesus and other great spiritual teachers made clear, there is a self that must be found and another that must be renounced. This teaching is found in each gospel (see Matt 10:39; 16:25; Mark 8:35; Luke 9:24), but is central to John's gospel, where it is coupled with "dying to the self": "unless a grain of wheat falls into the earth and dies, it remains just a single grain; but if it dies, it bears much fruit" (John 12:24). Hence, "those who love their life lose it [that is, their False Self], and those who hate their life [their False Self] in this world will keep it [their True Self] for eternal life" (John 12:25; see also 1 Cor 15:36–37, 42).

In one way or another, almost all religions say that we must die before we die—and then we will know what dying means, and what it does not mean. What it means, of course, is the relinquishment of selfish, possessive living, of egoic existence. The ego self is the self before death. Some form of death—psychological, spiritual, relational, or physical—is the only way we will loosen our ties to our small and separate False Self. Only then does it return in a new shape, which we call the soul, the True Self, or the Risen Christ.

There are four major splits from reality that we have all made in varying degrees to create our False Self:

- We split our mind from our body and soul, and live in our minds

- We split life from death and try to live without any "death"
- We split from our shadow self and pretend to be our idealized self
- We split ourselves from other selves and try to live apart, superior, and separate[1]

Each of these illusions must be overcome, either in this world or at the moment of physical death. Spirituality, pure and simple, is overcoming these splits from Reality. Anything less than the death of the False Self is inadequate religion. The False Self must die for the True Self to live, or, as Jesus put it, "If I do not go, the Advocate [the Holy Spirit] will not come to you" (John 16:7). Theologically speaking, what this verse is telling us is that Jesus (a good person) still had to die for the Christ (the universal presence) to arise. This is the pattern of transformation, where the letting go of the original indispensable self results in the arrival of a better reality.

Our True Self sees truthfully and will live forever. Our False Self is constantly changing and will eventually die. Our False Self is our necessary warm-up, our ego part that establishes our separate identity, especially in the first half of life. It is our incomplete self trying to pass for our whole self. The role of true spirituality, of mature religion, is to help speed up this process of dying to the False Self. Whatever one calls it, true spirituality is the form of living embodied by Jesus and taught by the Buddha. Such calm, egoless approach to life is invariably characteristic of people at the highest levels of doing and loving in all cultures and religions. These are the ones we call sages or holy ones.

Sometimes the end is the beginning, and the beginning points toward the end. As many poets and mystics have noted, the One Great Mystery is revealed at the beginning of our lives and forever beckons us toward its full realization. Many of us cannot let go of this implanted promise. Some call this homing device the soul, some call it the indwelling Holy Spirit, and others think of it as nostalgia or dreamtime. Whatever we call it, we cannot ignore it. It calls us both backward and forward, to our foundation and our future at the same time. The soul lives in such eternally deep time.

Speaking of this mystery, Richard Rohr notes that we are called forward by "a kind of deep homesickness," an inherent dissatisfaction that comes from our original and radical union with God.[2] Like loneliness, sadness, and depression, sickness, loss, and deprivation can serve as beacons to

---

1. Rohr, *Diamond*, 29.
2. The material in this segment is adapted from Rohr, *Falling Upward*, 65–96.

Death and Resurrection of the Self

light our way home. One of the reasons the *Wizard of Oz* has such lasting appeal is because Dorothy is guided forward to Oz and back to Kansas by her constant love and desire for home. Restlessness and dissatisfaction in life can serve as pointers to our destiny in God. The moment that we find ourselves in the presence of God is the moment we also find ourselves inside God.

The end was planted in us at the beginning, and it gnaws at us until we get there freely and consciously. Suffering, tragedy, and all episodes of loss in our lives are potentially sacramental. As Carl Jung put it, "when you stumble and fall, there you find pure gold." God hides, and is found, precisely in the depths of everything, especially so in the deep fathoming of our pain, suffering, weakness, and failure. This "something real" is what all the world religions point to when they speak of heaven, nirvana, bliss, or enlightenment. Their only mistake is to push it off into the next world. "If heaven comes later, it is because it is first of all now."[3]

How does God operate? We really don't know. But so many have encountered God in their weakness that we realize God's strength is God's ability to be patient, to refrain from overt use of power. From our perspective, then, we can say that God is a god of weakness, acting as much by persuasion as by direct action.

In tragedy and sickness, we are no longer in charge. That is good news, because all attempts to engineer or plan our own enlightenment are doomed to failure, since they are ego driven. The ego's job is to protect the status quo, so failure and humiliation force us to look beyond our comfort zones. Thus, we must stumble and fall. We must get out of the driver's seat for a while or we will never learn how to give up control to our soul's True Guide.

If we desire to grow spiritually, eventually some idea, event, or relationship will enter our life that we are not equipped to handle, using our present skill set. Richard Rohr calls such a situation a "stumbling stone," an event that causes you to leave your comfort zone in life.[4] Often such an experience involves physical or mental suffering. In this case, suffering will not solve any problem mechanically so much as it discloses the chronic problem in our lives, the refusal of our ego to let go. In such cases, suffering has a mentoring role, that of opening up new spaces within us for learning and loving. Francis of Assisi noted that when he kissed the leper, "what had been nauseating to me became sweetness and life." He marked that moment

3. Rohr, *Falling Upward*, 95.
4. Rohr, *Falling Upward.*, 68.

as his conversion, as the defining moment in his life, when he tasted his own insufficiency and began drawing from a different source.[5]

Learning How to See

As all mystics know and teach, spirituality is about seeing rightly, for "how one sees is what one sees." As Jesus says in Matthew 6:22, "The eye is the lamp of the body. So, if your eye is healthy, your whole body will be full of light." Moses could never have seen burning bushes as divine, could never have persevered with so much unknowing, unless he had moved to a higher level of seeing. William Blake, the seminal mystic poet who worked to bring about change both in the social order and in common ways of thinking, taught that "All we need to do is cleanse the doors of perception, and we shall see things as they are—infinite."

While Western religions have been preoccupied with telling people *what* to know and believe, mystics approach things differently, teaching people *how* to see. That, according to Luke's gospel, is what took place when the resurrected Jesus joined two ordinary travelers on their way home in Emmaus. He invites them to "open up" by telling their story of heartbreak. In the process, he explains to them his own life narrative. Through this act of intimacy and disclosure, they learn to see; their eyes are opened "and they recognized him" (Luke 24:31). Later that day, Jesus also appears to his sequestered disciples, transforming their vision from despondency to resurrection reality (Luke 24:36–49).

In the gospels, Jesus praises God for hiding divine wisdom "from the wise and the intelligent" and for having revealed it "to infants" (Matt 11:25). What is it that the learned and the clever often miss, and why is it that only infants and children see it? The learned and self-sufficient ones often see themselves as "having arrived," and by such arrogance, they remain outsiders to divine mystery. Their resistance and cleverness block its possibilities and hinder its reciprocity. Because of their vulnerability and dependence, children are avid learners, open to growth and newness. That is why children have a head start. When vulnerable exchange happens, there is always an augmentation of being on both sides. We are improved people afterward, bigger and better selves.

During the medieval period, two influential Christian philosophers at the monastery of St Victor in Paris—Hugh of St. Victor and Richard of

---

5. Rohr, *Falling Upward.*, 69–70.

St. Victor—wrote that humanity was given three different sets of eyes. The first was the eye of sensation, the second the eye of reason, and the third the eye of understanding. The third eye—the mystical gaze—builds on the first two, yet goes further. It represents the full goal of all seeing and knowing.

The first two ways of seeing, when separated from the third, result in dualistic thinking, an "us versus them" way of seeing, the foundation of much violence and discontent in the world. The third way of seeing—typifying the seer, the poet, the saint, and the authentic mystic—grasps the whole picture. Today's world has many eccentrics, fanatics, rebels, and self-promotors. What the world needs is more mystics who see with all three sets of eyes. Such people are both humble and compassionate, for knowing that they do not know, they experience the unknowable.

Some call such knowing conversion, some call it enlightenment, some transformation, and some holiness. This way of knowing is Paul's "third heaven," where he "heard things that are not to be told, that no mortal is permitted to repeat" (2 Cor 12:2–4). Far too often, organized religion has a stake in keeping members in the first or second heaven, for this keeps them coming back, and keeps clergy in business. This is not always intentional, but rather an extension of the principle that you can lead others only as far as you yourself have gone. Lacking the contemplative gaze, such leaders remain functionaries and technicians, their parishioners without the resources to guide them into Mystery. Theological training without spiritual experience is protectionist, not progressive.

What I call the contemplative gaze is not a technique for acquiring benefit, for getting ahead, or even a requirement for entry into heaven; nor is it a pious exercise that somehow pleases God. It is much more like practicing heaven now.

Paradoxically, if we misuse spiritual awareness, or keep it to ourselves, it "hides," and we cannot go deeper. This is why many remain at the level of mere "religion," and it is surely what Jesus means when he says, "For to those who have, more will be given, and they will have an abundance; but for those who have nothing, even what they have will be taken away" (Matt 13:12). How does the "secret" of God's kingdom, of God's reality and nature, become "unhidden"? It is disclosed when people stop hiding—from God, themselves, and others. The emergence of our True Self discloses the secret of God's kingdom, the mystery of reality.

All who witness this mystery, who experience its reality, "become children of God" (John 1:12), and, as Paul puts it, if children, then also "heirs of God and joint heirs with Christ" (Rom 8:15–17; see also Gal 4:7). While the Judeo-Christian tradition tells us we are already children of God, made in "God's image and likeness" (Gen 1:26–27), most of us have no clue what this means, and far fewer live out of its resources.

Twenty-five hundred years ago the Indian sage Siddhartha Gautama—the historical Buddha—experienced enlightenment. After years of training in the austerities of his native Hinduism, he was no closer to Truth than before he began. Then something changed. He took responsibility for his own awakening. He ceased to walk the path his teachers followed and simply sat down. He sat beneath a large fig tree in Bodh Gaya, India, and observed what he could of the world within and without. Then the veil lifted, and he realized what he was unable to see previously. Transformed, he knew what he was—he was awake.

Reading the Parables (and the Bible) with Nondual Eyes

In chapter 3, I discuss levels of consciousness and spirituality, emphasizing the difference between reading the Bible with dualist and nondualist eyes. How can we know the difference between these diametrically opposite ways of seeing, and how do we shift from one form of perception to the other? Thankfully, the computer era furnishes us with a whole set of new and wonderful images with which to envision the spiritual life. Like computers, we human beings come into existence with a specific operating system already installed in us. This default operating system, an egoic binary systems, runs on the power of "either/or." It comes by its dualism honestly, for the "binary operation" is built into the very structure of the human brain.

While a system based on duality has difficulty understanding or even appreciating nondual perspectives, it has the capacity to shift to an eventually different basis of perception. As we are now discovering, human beings come into this life with another operating system lying latent within us, and if we wish, we can upgrade from our egoic operating system (our False Self) to our deepest sense of identity (our True Self). This other operative system, often called the nondual or unitive system, is the operating system of the heart. It is this way of seeing and hearing, with the eyes and ears of the heart, that Jesus had in mind when he tells his disciples in Mark 4:11, "To you has been given the secret of the kingdom of God, but for those outside, everything comes in parables."

Death and Resurrection of the Self

In the Bible, as elsewhere in the wisdom tradition, the heart is primarily an organ of spiritual perception, the realm of meaning, value, conscience, and understanding. Unlike the egoic operating system, the heart does not perceive through differentiation. It doesn't divide reality into inside and out, subject and object. Rather, it perceives by means of harmony: all is subject; all is inside; all is holy. This seems to be what Jesus had in mind in his teachings. "Blessed are the pure [that is, the single] in heart, for they will see God," he says in the beatitudes (Matt 5:8). In these wisdom sayings, Jesus is not speaking of perfecting our virtue, but about upgrading our operating system. Jesus' entire mission can be seen as pushing, prodding, teasing, and shaking people beyond the limited understanding of their egoic operating system into the fastness of their fearless, compassionate, unitive humanity, or in other words, of their True Selves.

Christians aren't typically used to hearing that Jesus was focused on transforming their operating system. As we read scripture, we do so believing its message to be: try harder; be more hopeful, loving, and trusting; be a better version of yourself. In one of his parables, the enigmatic account of the Laborers in the Vineyard (Matt 20:1–16), Jesus speaks of the clash of operating systems in a way that is unmistakable.

Probably more than any other teaching in the gospels, this parable defies all logic and common sense. This is perhaps Jesus' most *koan*-like parable. Its teaching clearly contravenes our egoic operating system. The binary mind looks for consistency and fairness: equal pay for equal work! However, as the closing line of this parable indicates, this is a parable of reversal: "the last will be first, and the first will be last."

The only way to understand this parable, to "crack its code," is to shift our perspective and see the glass as half full rather than half empty. When we approach the story from the perspective of fullness, we see that there is enough for everyone, that well-being of each character is met, and that all along it had never been a question of competition. However, this kind of seeing is only accessible within the nondual operating system. Like any good Zen master, Jesus is not concerned with being nice, nor with wanting us to be nice also. Rather, he is out to short-circuit our mental wiring so that we are ushered into an entirely new way of seeing and being.

If this mindset is unsettling, the conclusion is even more disturbing: that until this mind shift has taken place, it is virtually impossible to live the teachings of Jesus. One of the ways traditional Christians have deluded themselves is in the sense that they have a franchise on the gospel, that they know how to live it or are somehow deserving or entitled, especially if they are privileged or comfortable. Every such expectation is a resentment waiting to happen. When we expect privilege, comfort, or convenience, we soon resent it when we don't get what we think we deserve. What the gospel tells us is "Stop expecting!" Entitlement is lethal for the soul. Everything is a gift—every moment, every day, every blessing. Only when we stop counting and figuring out what we deserve or what is fair will we move from this world of merit into the world of grace. And in the world of grace, everything is free.

As we stated earlier, Jesus was likely the first in the Middle or Near Eastern region to model this nondual or unitive teaching, and most of his followers, including the vast majority of his original disciples, missed it. The truth is that we cannot live nondual teaching with a dual mind. Until we are able to shift our operating system (both individually and collectively), we will only find ourselves in a position of hypocrisy, futility, and burnout.

Unfortunately, the path of Jesus has been attained by only a few Saint Francises and Mother Teresas of the world. The reason, to paraphrase the British writer G. K. Chesterton and the Indian sage Mohandas Gandhi, is not that Christianity is a failure, but that it has rarely been tried. When it is tried and attained, however, it is always in the same way: by exchanging the egoic operating system, with its inherent rigidity and fear, by the fullness of love that can be known only in and through the heart.

As Jesus indicates in John 16:12-13, "I still have many things to say to you, but you cannot bear them now. When the Spirit of truth comes, he will guide you into all truth." That Spirit is now here with us. We must get ready to take our place in the new spiritual order that is being revealed! Such changing of gears and engines from the first half of our lives does not happen without many slow realizations, inner calmings, lots of inner resistance and denials, and eventual surrenders.

To experience God's Spirit and the transformative power of the nondual operating system lying latent within us, I recommend two core spiritual practices to enhance or deepen this wisdom connection: Centering Prayer meditation (emptying the mind to make ourselves available to God), and lectio divina (a way of praying the scriptures). In many ways, these practices can function as living water for our souls, helping us bypass our "monkey mind" to enter more deeply into our heart (the center of our spiritual and emotional being), there to discover the living Christ.[6]

---

6. For a discussion of the meaning, intent, and methods of Centering Prayer and

Death and Resurrection of the Self

Kenotic Spirituality: Having the "Mind" of Christ

In contrast to virtually the whole of Christendom, with its vertical and hierarchical emphasis on spirituality—that the way to God is "up," moving from lower to higher—in the gospel of John Jesus emphasizes the horizontal process of interabiding: "Abide in me as I abide in you. Just as the branch cannot bear fruit by itself unless it abides in the vine, neither can you unless you abide in me. I am the vine, you are the branches. Those who abide in me and I in them bear much fruit" (15:4–5). I in you, you in me, all in God, God in all, that's the Fourth Gospel approach to spirituality. It is not a ladder but a circle that brings us to God: the continuously renewed giving and receiving that in its totality is where God dwells.

Kenotic spirituality (self-emptying as the path to fullness) is Jesus' unique and profoundly original contribution to the spiritual consciousness of humanity. Seeing Jesus' teachings, the message of scripture in general, as well Jesus himself and how we relate to God and others through this filter is both profoundly unsettling and profoundly hopeful; unsettling, because it dislodges us from our religious smugness, confidence, and dogmatism, but joyous in the sense that our heart knows this already, and joyous because the immediacy and spaciousness emerging from this new consciousness gives us the freedom to go deeper.

Underlying Jesus' teaching, and that of all scripture as well, is a call to a radical shift in consciousness, away from the alienation and polarization of the egoic operating system and into the unitive field of divine fullness that can only be perceived through the heart. Having this mindset is what the apostle Paul, quoting Isaiah 40:13, calls having "the mind of Christ" (1 Cor 2:16). As we noted in the previous chapter, it's one thing to theorize, but it's quite another to create this shift within oneself. This is where spiritual practice comes into place. There are many disciplines that help the emergence of the larger, nondual mind. While Jesus is typical of the wisdom tradition in his vision of what a whole and unified human being looks like, the route he laid out for getting there is altogether unique.

To understand this "road less taken," we go to Philippians 2:9–16, which contains an early Christian creedal hymn that describes "the mind of Christ" (Phil 2:5) acquired by the process of letting go or emptying oneself, summed up in the Greek word *kenosis*. In the Philippian hymn, Paul recognized that

---

lectio divina, consult the internet or books such as Beaurgeault's *Wisdom Jesus*, 141–60 and Vande Kappelle, *Potter's Workshop*, 77–93; 99–102.

everything Jesus did, he did by self-emptying—or, to put it another way, by the process of descent, taking the lower place, not the higher.

What makes this process effective is that it is almost completely spiritually counterintuitive. For the vast majority of the world's spiritual seekers, the way to God is up, or at least inward. Even in biblical tradition, the image of the spiritual ladder appears in Jacob's dream of a ladder going up to heaven (Gen 28:12, 17–18; see also John 1:51). The Christian monastic tradition returned to this image, and developed it further as essentially the roadmap for the spiritual journey. It is also central to rapture theology, in which Jesus' followers meet him "in the air" (1 Thess 4:17), continuing with him upward into heaven.

To rise requires insight and training, designed to harness spiritual energy—containing it rather than letting it dissipate. This ancient and universal strategy underlies all genuine asceticism and spiritual devotion. And it works for some modern people as well. However, such a strategy requires increasingly higher and more intense effort, and it can lead to futility, resignation, or self-destruction.

As Jesus indicates, there is another route to the center, a coherent and more powerful path of inner transformation, achieved not through storing up or concentrating spiritual energy, but by letting it go—or by giving it away. Unitive consciousness is reached not through effort, attainment, or the concentration of being, but through self-emptying—not through "up" but through "down." This is the way of kenosis, the revolutionary path that Jesus introduced into the consciousness of the West through his parabolic teaching. This is the way, not only of Jesus Christ, but of God, who so loved the world that he gave himself on its behalf. In the work of the modern Roman Catholic theologian Karl Rahner, "God is the prodigal who squanders himself." Jesus' act of letting go or self-emptying (embodied in his manner of life as well as in his manner of death), is simply related to God's original act of creating, described in Genesis 1 as "letting be," and it was through God's original "Let there be" that our visible universe emerged.

The great Sufi poet Jallaludin Rumi (1207–1273) expressed the concept of self-emptying and letting go in these beautiful lines:

> I died as a mineral and became a plant
> I died as a plant and rose to animal,
> I died as an animal and I was man.
> Why should I fear? When was I less by dying?[7]

7. Quoted from Sara Sviri, *Taste of Hidden Things*, 210.

Death and Resurrection of the Self

Jesus certainly called his followers to die to self, but his idea of dying to self was not through inner renunciation or guarding the purity of his being, but through radically squandering everything he had and was. John the Baptist's disciples were horrified because Jesus banqueted, drank, and danced. The Pharisees were horrified because he healed on the sabbath and kept company with women and disreputables, people known to be impure. Boundaries meant nothing to him; he walked right through them.

Abundance and generosity bordering on extravagance seemed to be the signatures of both his teaching and his personal style. This was a quality displayed not only in teachings such as the parable of the Unforgiving Servant (Matt 18:22–34) and of the Laborers in the Vineyard (Matt 20:1–15), which emphasize what can only be perceived as "unfair" behavior, but also in his miracles. For example, when he feeds the multitudes at the Sea of Galilee, there is not merely enough to go around, but the leftovers fill twelve baskets (Matt 14:20). When a woman anoints him with expensive ointment and the disciples grumble about the waste, Jesus seems not to count the cost, and even forbids counting the cost (Matt 26:13).

Regarding his motto concerning goods and possessions, one could argue that Jesus' motto was "do not hoard" or "do not cling," not even to life itself (Luke 12:32). All will come of its own accord in good time and with abundant fullness, so long as one does not attempt to hoard or cling. This is a path he walked to the very end. In the garden of Gethsemane, with his betrayers and accusers gathering at the gates, he struggled and anguished but remained true to his course: "Not my will but yours be done" (Luke 22:42). Thus he came and thus he went, giving himself fully into life and death, losing himself, squandering himself. It was not love stored up but love utterly poured out that characterized his life.

Over and over, Jesus lays this path before us as well. Everything can be embraced, but the catch is to cling to nothing. You let things go, picking up nothing, clinging to nothing, sticking to nothing, yet willing to give his life on behalf of others. That's the kenotic path in a nutshell; so simply, so gracious, yet so costly. This was not the first time such spirituality had been taught, but when Jesus taught and lived it, it was still a concept so far ahead of its time that even his close disciples couldn't grasp it, and if they did, they couldn't quite stay with it. Paul caught it perfectly in his kenotic hymn, but then lost it in the long lists of rules and moral injunctions that dominate his epistles. And as the church took shape as an institution, it could not exceed the wingspan of its first apostolic teachers, for what they did not fully understand, they were unable accurately to transmit. Thus, right from the start the radical simplicity of Jesus' nondual kenotic path tended to get swallowed up by older and more familiar forms of legalistic effort and righteousness.

Despite the long lineage of people who didn't quite get the path that Jesus was teaching, in the fourth century there arose in Cappadocia (modern-day southern Turkey) a wisdom school led by three profoundly wise teachers called Basil of Caesarea, Gregory of Nyssa, and Gregory of Nazianzus. Among their many contributions, these Cappadocian teachers came to understand the three members of the Trinity not merely as "God in three persons" but as a state of being characterized by self-emptying love. As they viewed it, the three persons of the Trinity were involved in a constant outpouring of love from Father to Son, Son to Spirit, and Spirit back to Father. And the word they used to describe these mutual outpourings is *perichoresis*, which literally means "the dance around." The profound insight here is that God reveals his own innermost nature through a continuous dance of self-emptying, thus bringing the statement "God is love" into its full reality. Contemporary theologians such as the Spanish scholar Raimon Panikkar and the Franciscan teacher Richard Rohr both have made *perichoresis* the cornerstone of their teaching in describing how God's love moves and flows as the unified field of all reality.

Jesus' teaching assures us as we move along the reckless and in some ways abundant and extravagant downward or outward kenotic pathway that divine love is infinite and immediate and will always come to us if we don't cling. As we practice in daily life, in acts of compassion, kindness, and self-emptying, both at the level of our doing and even more at the level of our being, something is catalyzed out of that self-emptying. Subtle qualities of divine love essential to the well-being of this planet are released through our actions and flow out into the world as miracle, healing, and hope. And the template for that divine alchemy is imprinted in our soul and has always been there in the hidden dynamism of love. This, I believe, is the path that Jesus taught and walked, the path he called and still calls his followers to walk.

Jesus was the first truly integral teacher to appear on this planet. As we take a fresh look at Jesus' parabolic teachings at once familiar and strange, we are catapulted forward along a path that rings with the power of truth.

Death and Resurrection of the Self

Questions for Discussion and Reflection

Having read chapter 4, answer the following questions, writing your answers in a journal. If you are in a group study, be prepared to share your answers with those in the group.

1. Assess the merit of the author's statement that life's greatest adventure—its greatest game and challenge—is the spiritual transformation of one's self.
2. Assess the validity of the notion that humans possess both a False and a True Self.
3. What does the author mean by the True Self? How is the True Self related to God?
4. Explain the relationship between one's ego and one's False Self.
5. Explain the relationship between one's soul and one's True Self.
6. Explain how the False Self sees everything in parts and how the True Self sees everything in wholes.
7. Assess the merit of Carl Jung's statement that "when you stumble and fall, there you find true gold." Do you agree with the author's view that encounter with God occurs more in one's weakness than in one's strength? Explain your answer.
8. In our journey from our False Self to our True Self, what is the role of the "stumbling stone"?
9. In spiritual consciousness (as well as in reading scripture), explain the distinction between knowing and seeing, that is, between seeing and hearing with the mind and seeing and hearing with the heart.
10. After reading this chapter, what did you learn about discipleship as having the "mind" of Christ?
11. After reading this chapter, what did you learn about interabiding?
12. In practical terms, explain the meaning of *perichoresis*.
13. Are you satisfied with your current spiritual state? If not, where would you like to head spiritually, and what adjustments do you need to get there?

5

The Nature of Scripture

WHY DO PEOPLE READ scripture? What is its function in the lives of believers? People read the Bible for many reasons: literarily (as great literature), philosophically (as a guide for moral and reflective thought), theologically (as a compendium of truth), or devotionally (as a resource for meditation and a source of comfort). Despite the Bible's widespread scriptural use, most devout people read it only occasionally, and superficially. How people read it is perhaps more important than why they read it. For those who wish to engage with scripture seriously and in depth, I recommend that you find a method of study that works for you, whether individually or with others, and commit to it. Of many valid ways of reading scripture, the following are recommended:

- Reading for *information*—to learn as much as possible about the setting of the authors and their primary audience in order to discover the original meaning of a particular passage of scripture and its potential application.

- Reading for *formation*—to establish one's identity, values, and beliefs in order to live meaningfully, joyously, and securely.

- Reading for *transformation*—to provide resources for developing soulcentrically rather than egocentrically, aligning more deeply with one's powers of nurturing and creating, presence and wonder.

Of course, it is quite possible for these approaches to overlap, due to the complexity of our intellectual, theological, and spiritual needs. It is

The Nature of Scripture

equally possible that biblical passages convey messages appropriate to our varied abilities and needs. Scripture is multivalent, meaning that it's message allows for multiple interpretations. While one text might strike terror in the heart of an unrepentant person, the same passage might exhort devout believers to greater faithfulness and even greater freedom. When you read any book or section of the Bible, particularly in a group setting, keep in mind the possibility that biblical passages contain multiple messages, depending on one's needs, temperament, and spiritual journey. Scripture, like a good smorgasbord, provides healthy options for different appetites. And you don't always have to eat the same food; sometimes a change of diet can be helpful.

As Paul showed in 1 Corinthians, the important thing is to keep growing spiritually. Paul's concern with the Corinthians was that they were in a state of spiritual immaturity, unable to eat solid food. It takes time—and conscious effort—to grow spiritually, from egocentrism to soulcentrism. How people hear and read scripture (eat spiritually) reflects their spiritual maturity.

Perhaps you have heard it said that the modern age has problems with authority in general, and with the authority of scripture in particular. However, according to 2 Timothy 3:16, the Bible should not be considered as an authority in the modern sense of the word; in other words, the Bible does not exist for its own sake. Note that this passage does not say, "All scripture is inspired by God and is *authoritative*." It says that all scripture is inspired and *useful*—useful to teach, rebuke, correct, instruct, and equip us for our mission as the people of God. For too long we have read the Bible as if it were God's encyclopedia, God's rule book, God's answer book, God's scientific text, God's easy-steps instruction book, God's little book of morals for all occasions. In Jesus' day, the only people who would have had anything close to these expectations of the Bible would have been the scribes and Pharisees. And Jesus certainly disapproved of their attitudes and methodology regarding scripture.

While the Hebraic scriptures (the Old Testament) provide codes of behavior and belief that can be systematized into groups of tens or twelves, the canonical writings of Christianity intentionally fail to do so, even for religious matters. To the question, "What does the New Testament teach on X or Y?" the proper answer seems, "What did you read last in the New Testament?" The New Testament is not a collection of books that provides a system of law for personal or public behavior, but rather a way of life based on discernment and wisdom, subjecting morality under fuzzy topics such as "love," "mercy," and "forgiveness."

When you let go of the Bible as God's answer book, you get it back as something so much better. It becomes the family story—the story of the people who have been called by the one true God to be his agents in the world, to be his servants to the rest of the world. So I suggest we stop reading the Bible as a "modern" answer book. But that doesn't mean we should discard it. Just the opposite! When we let it go as a modern answer book, we get to rediscover it for what it really is: an ancient book of incredible spiritual value for us, a kind of universal and cosmic history, a book that tells us who we are and what story we find ourselves in so that we know what to do and how to live. Of course, the Bible is even more than a book of wisdom and wisdom development. It is a book that calls together and helps create a community, a community that is a catalyst for God's work in our world.

In his intriguing fable, *A New Kind of Christian*, Brian McLaren criticizes modern liberals and conservatives alike for reading the Bible in very modern ways. Modern conservatives treat the Bible as if it were a modern book. They are used to reading modern history texts, modern encyclopedias, modern science articles, and modern legal codes, and so they assume that the Bible will yield its resources if they approach it like one of those texts. However, none of those categories even existed when the Bible was written. Sure, there was history, but not with all of the modern trimmings like a concern for factual accuracy, corroborating evidence, or absolute objectivity. There was law, but surely not a one-to-one correspondence between ancient Near Eastern concepts of law and our modern concept. The conservatives seem somewhat blind to these kinds of differences. Modern liberals seem to make a corresponding mistake. Acknowledging that the Bible is a different kind of text from our modern texts, they still judge it by modern standards. If something doesn't fit in with a modern Western mindset that reveres objectivity, science, democracy, individualism, and the like, they dismiss it as primitive and irrelevant.[1]

There is a third option: instead of reading the Bible, what if you let the Bible read you? If that sounds a bit ethereal, perhaps even mystical, think of it this way. Think of a scientist preparing to dissect a frog, or think of a detective at a crime scene. How would you describe their attitude or approach? Now think of a teenage girl meeting a boy at the mall. Surely her attitude differs from the scientist's or the detective's. Her approach wouldn't

---

1. McLaren, *New Kind of Christian*, 55–56.

be so analytical or objective. And there would be some fun in it, a sense of personal investment, a feeling of adventure. In one sense, there's less caution, less holding back. Yet in another way, there is holding back, because she wants to make her move and then leave room for him to respond. This approach is less aggressive, less controlling, and more relational. We need to approach the Bible that way; we need to flirt with it, romance it—or possibly let its message romance us.[2]

Our modern age has predisposed us to only a limited range of postures with the Bible, like the objective analysis of a scientist or like forensic science, always trying to prove something. It's all about conquering the text, reducing it to something explainable by our preconceptions, turning it into moralisms, principles, outlines, conclusions, or proofs. What would happen if we approached the text less aggressively but even more energetically and passionately? What would happen if we honestly listened to the story and put ourselves under its spell, so to speak, not using it to get all of our questions about God answered but instead trusting it to pose questions about us. What would happen if we simply trusted ourselves to it—the way we fall in love, or fall asleep?

Christianity is centered in the Bible. Of course, it is ultimately centered in God, but it is the God of whom the Bible speaks and to whom it points. God may be known in other ways and through other religions, but to be Christian is to be centered in the God of the Bible. This is not a mark of Christian exclusion, but of Christian identity. The Bible is for Christians their sacred scripture, their sacred story.[3]

Yet the Bible has become a stumbling block for many. In the last half century, many Christians have left the church because of the Bible. More precisely, they left because the traditional literal way of interpreting the Bible, with its emphasis on biblical infallibility, historical factuality, and moral and doctrinal absolutes, became intolerable. In his writings, biblical scholar Marcus Borg provides an alternative to biblical literalism. Utilizing three adjectives—*historical, metaphorical*, and *sacramental*—he describes how scripture, creeds, and other normative Christian teachings should be understood.[4]

---

2. McLaren, *New Kind of Christian*, 56–57.
3. Borg, *Heart of Christianity*, 43.
4. This segment appears in many of my commentaries and I use it again here because of its usefulness. It is adapted from Borg's *Heart of Christianity*, 43–60.

Living Water

To speak of *the Bible as a historical product* is to see that it is a human product, not a divine product. Not "absolute truth" but relatively and culturally conditioned, the Bible uses the language and concepts of the cultures in which it took shape. It tells us how our spiritual ancestors saw things, not how God sees things. The Bible is not verbally inspired, since the emphasis is not upon words inspired by God but on people moved by their experience of God.

For modern Christians, describing the Bible as sacred scripture and therefore as "holy" is to value the historical process known as canonization. The documents that make up the Bible were not "sacred" when they were written, but over time were declared sacred, meaning that they became the most important documents for that community, providing its foundation and shaping its identity.

Much of the language of the Bible is metaphorical: one third of the Old Testament is poetry or semi-poetical literature. To speak of *the Bible as metaphor* is to emphasize that this language should not be interpreted literally. Metaphor does not mean that the Bible is not true, but rather that it is not primarily concerned with facticity. The Bible does contain history, but even when a text contains historical memory, its meaning is more than (not less than) literal. For example, although the exile in Babylon in the sixth century BCE really happened, the way the story is told gives it a more than historical meaning. It became a metaphorical narrative of exile and return, providing images of the human condition and its remedy. In other cases, as the Genesis stories of creation, there may be little or no historical factuality. Though these stories are not literally factual, they are profoundly true.

Because the gospels combine memory and metaphor, some of these accounts, when literalized, become literally incredible. The story of Jesus walking on water illustrates the point. A literal reading of the story emphasizes the spectacular event as a sign of Jesus's identity, "proof" that he was divine. A metaphorical reading of this story yields a different meaning. It seems to be a way of saying: "Here in a nutshell is what the story of Jesus is about."

Historically speaking, the gospel accounts do not begin with what Jesus said and did before his death. Christianity begins with the experience of Jesus after his death by his followers. They write of him as one resurrected from the dead and exalted to God's presence. Accounts of his birth and transfiguration, of his feeding the multitudes, restoring sight to the blind, turning water into wine, raising the dead, and walking on the water, all are

The Nature of Scripture

resurrection stories! The gospel accounts are all told from the perspective of resurrection, of victory over death. The evangelists are not writing about an ordinary human, but rather about one who is already viewed as Lord, Messiah, and preexistent Christ.

A metaphorical reading of the gospels provides rich meaning for Christians in all times and places; a literal reading misses all of this, emphasizing belief in the miraculous elements rather than on its meaning for a life of faith. Metaphorical language is *a way of seeing*. To apply this to the Bible means that in addition to its metaphorical language and metaphorical narratives, the Bible as a whole may be thought of as a "giant" metaphor. "Thus the point is not to believe in the Bible—but to see our lives with God through it."[5]

To speak of *the Bible as sacrament* is to say that it mediates the sacred. If a sacrament is a physical vehicle or vessel for the Spirit, the Bible is sacrament in the sense that it is a visible human product whereby God becomes present to us.

For modern Christians, "the Bible—human in origin, sacred in status and function—is both metaphor and sacrament. As metaphor, it is a way of seeing—a way of seeing God and our life with God. As sacrament, it is a way that God speaks to us and comes to us."[6] The Bible is a two-way bridge, a path to the divine and a way to connect to our deepest self. Like a backboard in the game of basketball, scripture is a means to an end, not an end in itself.

While the Bible functions as a rule book or as God's answer book for many Jews and Christians, it is primary great literature. Hence, we should not be surprised to find that at the heart of the Hebrew scriptures (the Old Testament)—essential to its teaching and exhortation—we find story, song (psalms and hymns), and proverb. Likewise, at the heart of Christianity's scripture (the New Testament)—essential to its teaching and exhortation—we find story, song (creedal hymns and prayers), and parable.

A Parabolic Approach to Scripture

Within the Hebraic tradition, there were two unique categories or offices of religious authority, that of priest or prophet. However, within the spiritual traditions of the wider ancient East (including Judaism), there was also a

---

5. Borg, *Heart of Christianity*, 57.
6. Borg, *Heart of Christianity*, 59.

third, the teacher of wisdom, one who taught the ancient traditions of the transformation of the human being. These teachers of transformation, which included the authors of Hebrew wisdom literature such as Ecclesiastes, Job, and Proverbs, were likely the early precursors to the rabbi, whose task it was to interpret the law and lore of Judaism. The hallmark of these wisdom teachers was their use of aphorisms, riddles, and parables rather than prophetic pronouncements or divine decree. They spoke to people in the language common to the masses, the language of story rather than of law.

Parables are a wisdom genre. According to Episcopal priest, teacher, and author Cynthia Bourgeault, parables "belong to *mashal*, the Jewish branch of the universal tradition of sacred poetry, stories, proverbs, riddles, and dialogues through which wisdom is conveyed. . . . We can see the razor edge of [Jesus'] brilliance as he takes the familiar world of *mashal* far beyond the safety zone of conventional morality into a world of radical reversal and paradox. He is transforming proverbs into parables—and a parable, incidentally, is not the same thing as an aphorism or a moral lesson. Its closest cousin is really the Buddhist *koan*, a deliberately subversive paradox aimed at turning our usual mind upside down. . . . Their job is not to confirm but to uproot. You can imagine the effect that had on his audience! Throughout the gospels we hear people saying again and again, 'What is this he's teaching? No one has ever said anything like this before. Where did he get this? Where did he come from?'"[7]

Stories were Jesus' stock-in-trade, the primary medium by which he conveyed his message. The parables occupy fully 35 percent of the first three gospels, as well as of the gospel of John, if we consider the parabolic nature of the similitudes or "I–Am sayings" found in that gospel. One of the most surprising features of Jesus' parables is that they are not primarily about God. They are about weddings and banquets, family relations, muggings, farmers sowing and reaping, and about shrewd business dealings. Obviously, Jesus wanted us to look closely at this world, not some other one. It is here and now—all around us in the most ordinary things—that we find the divine presence.

While similar to Zen *koans* in some ways, Jesus' stories were also different in important respects. While the Zen stories aim at changing one's perception of the world, Jesus wanted people to see that the world itself was changing, and that therefore they had better change the way they looked at it. He invited them, in effect, to become part of the change. Time after time

---

7. Beaurgeault, *Wisdom Jesus*, 23–24, 27.

The Nature of Scripture

he said, "They that have eyes to see, let them see, and they that have ears, let them hear." He simply wanted people to pay attention to what was going on around them and to discern a reality that required wisdom to perceive. To describe this change, Jesus used a term that his listeners would have found familiar, though they might have been startled by the way he used it. He called it the coming of the "kingdom of God." What he meant was that something was happening, not just in the consciousness of the listener, but also in the world itself. Something new and unprecedented was happening, and they could be a part of it.[8]

What I am suggesting in *Living Water* is not simply the centrality of parables to Jesus, but also that our very way of reading and interpreting scripture be parabolic as well, its intent not to confirm but to uproot, not to make us feel cozy or safe but to challenge us to ongoing personal transformation.

Questions for Discussion and Reflection

Having read chapter 5, answer the following questions, writing your answers in a journal. If you are in a group study, be prepared to share your answers with those in the group.

1. Describe the role of scripture in your upbringing or faith tradition.
2. Do you read the Bible primarily for information, formation, or transformation? Explain your answer.
3. Explain what is meant by the polyvalence or multivalence of scripture. If possible, provide examples of your discovery of multiple interpretations of a biblical verse, passage, or doctrine.
4. Assess the merit of Brian McLaren's view that rather than us reading the Bible, we should let the Bible read us? Have you had this experience with the Bible? If so, provide an example.
5. Assess Marcus Borg's three alternatives to biblical literalism, that is, his emphasis on reading the Bible historically, metaphorically, and sacramentally. Which of these do you consider most important or appealing? Explain your answer.
6. What do Christians generally mean when they say that the Bible is "holy"? Does the word "sacred" necessarily imply anything supernatural about the origin or nature of scripture? Explain your answer.

8. Cox, Harvey, *When Jesus Came to Harvard*, 155, 159.

7. Assess the merit of reading and interpreting the Bible "literally."
8. Assess the merit of the statement that gospel accounts of the life, ministry, and death of Jesus are essentially "resurrection stories."
9. Assess the merit of equating Jesus' parables with Jewish wisdom forms such as proverbs and riddles.
10. Assess the merit of equating Jesus' parables with Buddhist *koans*.
11. Assess the merit of the author's suggestion that we approach scripture in a parabolic way.

6

The Nature of Jesus' Teaching

HAD JESUS NO OTHER legacy, he would be remembered as one of the world's master teachers. "Teacher" was a title even his enemies were willing to concede to him. When they approached him with a testing question, they began by saying, "Teacher, we know that you are sincere, and teach the way of God in accordance with truth" (Matt 22:16; Mark 12:14; Luke 20:21).

The gospels use three Greek titles to describe Jesus as teacher. The most common is *didaskalos* (teacher, master), used of Jesus almost forty times. Luke also uses the word *epistatēs* (chief, master, lord), a term that in secular Greek would have been used for a headmaster. Sometimes the gospel writers employ the title rabbi, the standard Jewish title for a distinguished and acknowledged teacher. When we put the three titles together, knowing that they all represent the word rabbi, the customary word for an accepted teacher, we find that the four gospels call Jesus "teacher" more than fifty times. The New Testament thus presents us with the picture of Jesus as a master teacher, a teacher par excellence.

All great teachers possess three qualities: (a) mastery of a subject, (b) mastery of communication, and (c) ability to practice what they teach. Jesus excelled in each—in knowledge, ability, and practice. Jesus did not come on the scene of first-century Judaism, however, to conform to anyone's preconceived expectations about sages, or for that matter, about prophets or messiahs. His subject, essentially, was threefold: he came to make known something about God, something about humankind, and something about their interrelationship.

Living Water

In Jesus' day there was a vast human quest for God, wrapped up in piety and legalism (Judaism) and in idolatry and superstition (Gentiles). The Jews were monotheists and had a central temple in Jerusalem, dedicated to sacrifice and rituals. Much of their worship was motivated by duty and regulated by tradition. While there were undoubtedly devout priests and religious leaders, many were corrupt. Despite good rabbis and moral leaders, teaching excellent maxims and pure precepts, many were ineffectual (see Matt 7:28–29). However good their intention, their efforts failed to reach the human heart.

Jesus began his teaching by speaking of God as Father, as one who could only be approached through spiritual worship (John 4:23–24). When Jesus revealed God's character as Love (John 3:16), all existing worship, whether pagan or monotheistic, came under question as misguided or inadequate. Under Jesus' guidance, for the first time worshippers could address the Creator of the world as *abba* (Mark 14:36; see Rom 8:15; Gal 4:6), meaning "Daddy" or "Father." A greater understanding of God, a more transformative perspective, has never been imparted.

His words, a mirror into the character of God, likewise penetrated the secrets of the human heart. According to John's gospel, never did one understand human thought and motivation as Jesus. After spending time with Jesus, the Samaritan woman could but testify: "He told me everything I have ever done!" (John 4:29, 39). When the Samaritans came and heard for themselves, they too agreed (John 4:42). When Jesus spoke, people did not just listen; they followed! (Mark 2:13–14). Where did he gain such knowledge, ability, and wisdom? Surely not from parents, school, or other rabbis.

From what we know, there was not a single precept that Jesus did not exhibit in his own conduct. He enjoined meekness, humility, self-denial, temperance, gratitude, prudence, generosity, forgiveness, and deeds of mercy, not only to those who could respond in kind, but also to the unlovable, even to one's enemy. As known by his followers and remembered by tradition, his character was pure and blameless, his motive sincere, his compassion and love unbounded. No one before had seen such a human, but those who knew him would agree with Nicodemus: "Rabbi, we know that you are a teacher who has come from God" (John 3:2).

Jesus seems to have begun his teaching in the synagogues of Galilee, but before long, whether due to opposition by religious authorities or to popularity or both, by far the greater part of his teaching occurred outdoors. Such teaching requires an engaging style, otherwise he would

The Nature of Jesus' Teaching

not have gathered an audience, or retained it. In the gospels we find him teaching in the streets and on the roads, sometimes using a boat by the seashore, holding the crowd spellbound. We find him engaged in technical arguments and discussion with the scholars of his day, even teaching the crowds gathered in the temple precinct at Jerusalem. He was equally effective amidst the crowds as within the intimate inner circle of his disciples. Such diversity of audience and setting required universal appeal.

To be arresting, universal in appeal, and intellectually intelligible requires another capacity, the ability to be permanently memorable. How did he accomplish this task? Through a combination of forms such as picturesque speech, paradoxical statements, puns, proverbs, and parables. Think of the beatitudes (Matt 5:1–16; Luke 6:20–26), statements if taken literally sound incredible, but that somehow haunt the mind and heart with the sense that, given time, they contain great truth: "Blessed are the poor, the hungry, the sorrowful, the persecuted." Each beatitude contradicts the world's standards, reverses worldly wisdom, turns life upside down. Or consider the statement that unless adults change and become like children, they will never enter God's domain (Matt 18:3). One such sentence from the mouth of Jesus annihilates current standards of prestige and greatness. The great value of such sayings is their penetrating power, their ability to linger long after their first hearing. In many ways Jesus was the great disturber, not least in these thought-provoking paradoxes.

Along with his contemporaries, Jesus delighted in sharp contrasts and extreme statements, in hyperbole and exaggeration. His teaching was characterized, not by greys and halftones, but by bold contrasting colors. Note the colorful speech he used in Matthew 7:3–5 to point out ludicrous behavior: "Why do you see the speck in your neighbor's eye, but do not notice the log in your own eye?" Jesus uses extreme imagery to say in a powerful and memorable way what most people would express tritely as "Why are you acting inconsistently?"

By taking into account the presence of vivid hyperbole in Jesus' teaching, we can sometimes avoid misinterpreting the meaning of certain hard saying in the gospels. For example, the passage in Luke 14:26 about the necessity of "hating" one's family in order to become a follower of Jesus is best understood in light of the use of exaggeration so common in the Middle Eastern culture of that time. Obviously, Jesus had no desire to increase the sum total of hatred in the world. An examination of the parallel statement in Matthew 10:37 shows that Jesus did not come to increase hatred but to increase love for God and loyalty to himself as their teacher.

A word of caution is appropriate, however, against attempting to find exaggeration in the teachings of Jesus where the statement is to be taken literally. We must be careful not to dilute uncompromising statements simply because we find them extreme or demanding. For example, Jesus' command to the rich man who inquired what he should do to inherit eternal life, "Sell all that you own and distribute the money to the poor . . . then come, follow me" (Luke 18:22), should not be taken as hyperbole. As the context makes clear, the questioner understood Jesus' words literally.

Wisdom Language and Imagery in the New Testament

The study of Jewish wisdom literature as found in the Hebrew Bible (Old Testament) and in the intertestamental literature provides readers of the New Testament with an important and intriguing perspective on Jesus and early Christianity. Following the resurrection of Jesus, when early Christians were looking for language and concepts to express their experience and understanding of Jesus, one of the most helpful resources was the Jewish wisdom literature. Of course, other parts of the Hebrew Bible were valuable, such as the prophets, the psalms, and the historical traditions of Israel, but the authors of the New Testament and the leaders of the early Christian communities saw in the wisdom literature, particularly in the books of Sirach and Wisdom, important resources for understanding Jesus and their new life in Christ.

In *Jesus the Sage*, Ben Witherington divides early Jewish wisdom into two major traditions: conventional wisdom (as found in Proverbs and Sirach) and counter-order wisdom (as found in Ecclesiastes and Job). He maintains that through his teaching and way of life Jesus modeled the latter tradition, particularly in his parables and aphorisms of reversal (as exemplified by his care for weak and marginalized individuals).

If we are correct in assuming that sages constituted a distinct class within Israel, primarily as teachers of Jewish youth, we may also assume that they used a characteristic mode of discourse. The introduction to the book of Proverbs (1:6) mentions four kinds of sapiential teaching that students must understand: (1) the *proverb* or *mashal*. This short, pithy statement, a basic similitude or likeness in which a given phenomenon is compared or contrasted alongside another, is expressed through the Hebraic feature of parallelism. There are three major types of parallelism. The simplest is called synonymous parallelism, where the second half of the line repeats the thought of the first with a slight variation (see Prov 4:11). Antithetic parallelism contrasts ideas (see Prov 10:7) while the third type, synthetic parallelism, advances an idea and moves it toward a new concept (see Prov 16:31); (2) the *parable* (a saying or narrative conveying an important message hidden within a clever formulation); (3) the *"wise saying"* or aphorism (a general category or collection of sapiential instruction); and (4) the *riddle* (an enigmatic saying leading to reflection on the meaning of life and its inequities). While no pure riddles have survived within biblical wisdom literature, there can be little doubt that ancient sages coined enigmas and that the solving of riddles belonged to the essential tasks of the wise. All of the above use admonitions and warnings as powerful expressions of cultural truth.

The Jewish wisdom tradition profoundly influenced the New Testament community. Wisdom images and ideas appear in every layer of the New Testament, from the letter of James, a document of early Christianity best understood as Jewish Christian sapiential writing, to the gospels, which portray Jesus as a wisdom teacher, to the letters of Paul, where Christ is called the wisdom of God (1 Cor 1:24). Wisdom traditions influenced the document called "Q," an early sayings source that circulated independently and is believed to have been used by the authors of the gospels of Matthew and Luke. This source, whether oral or written, consisted mainly of Jesus' teachings. While drawing on diverse genres, the majority of the sayings in Q are wisdom sayings, which portray Jesus as a sage or teacher of sapiential truth.

The first three gospels in the New Testament are called "synoptic" because they draw from one another and look at Jesus with similar eyes. In all three, Jesus is portrayed as a wisdom teacher, displaying a style of instruction similar to that of the sages, teaching disciples through parables (narrative proverbs or *meshalim*) and wisdom sayings (aphorisms) that tease the mind.

In the teaching of Jesus there is no feature more striking than his parables. Whether we consider their literary features or according to their influence in human life, they are incomparable. They have supplied inspiration to poets, artists, moralists, philosophers, theologians, and public speakers. Many expressions used commonly today come from Jesus' parables. Most of us know what is meant by "hiding one's lamp under a bushel" or "being a good Samaritan." No one had previously spoken of natural abilities as "talents" until Jesus told his parable of the Talents; the original meaning of talent referred to a certain measure or weight of gold and silver.

The old definition of a parable as "an earthly story with a heavenly meaning" contains some truth, but one must beware against seeking elaborate allegorical meaning in every parable. A turning point in the study of Jesus' parables came in the 1880s and 1890s when the German biblical scholar Adolf Jülicher (1857–1938) introduced his "one-point" approach to parable interpretation. Since then, the proper method of interpreting Jesus' parables has been to make a thorough inquiry into the "life-setting" in his ministry when he first uttered the parable, and to seek out the main point it was intended to teach. On the whole, the details are seen to provide little more than background and should not be assigned allegorical meaning. This approach to Jesus' parables reveals that most were intended to perform one of four functions: (1) to portray a human trait or character for our warning or example (in other words, to teach a form of conduct that Jesus' followers should either emulate or avoid); (2) to disclose a principle of God's providential rule in the world (that is, to reveal something of the character of God and God's dealings with humanity); (3) to depict a truth about how Jesus' followers are to relate to others and to society at large; and (4) to provide warning or preparation for the future (namely, to speak of future judgment and preparedness for entrance into God's kingdom).

Our approach, based on more recent scholarship, expands this interpretive matrix. While the traditional functions of parables hold merit and are applicable in specific parables, the ensuing chapters develop a case for a wisdom approach to the parables, arguing that they are intended to force the reader or listener to deeper levels of consciousness, requiring transformation from one's False Self to one's True Self.

Jesus as Jewish "Prophetic Sage"

It is possible to argue that the Jesus tradition (Jesus material found in the New Testament and espoused by the first Christians) is the next logical development of the Jewish wisdom tradition. The New Testament draws on the entirety of that tradition, particularly on Sirach (Ecclesiasticus) and the book of Wisdom (Wisdom of Solomon), intertestamental books read by Christians familiar with the Septuagint (books found in Roman Catholic and Eastern Orthodox Bibles but excluded from most Protestant Bibles).

The Nature of Jesus' Teaching

The gospels introduce Jesus as a Jewish prophetic sage who communicates primarily in wisdom forms of utterance and who, like great Jewish sages before him, cross-fertilizes them with sapiential adaptation of prophetic and legal forms of utterance. What makes the category of "sage" most appropriate for describing Jesus is that he either casts his teaching in recognizable sapiential forms (aphorism, beatitude, or riddle) or else uses the prophetic adaptation of sapiential speech—the parable (narrative *mashal*). In either case, he speaks figuratively, addressing his audience with indirect speech. This teaching style makes Jesus enigmatic, particularly for modern people who value communication based on self-evident propositions and syllogistic logic.

The majority of authentic Jesus sayings are either aphorisms (*meshalim*) or parables (narrative *meshalim*). It is important to note that Jesus never used the classic prophetic formula, "thus says the Lord." The closest approximation of this formula is in a Q saying found in Luke 11:49: "Therefore also the Wisdom of God said." As this passage indicates, Jesus' chosen way to communicate is the way of a sage, persuading by indirect and figurative speech. Scholars estimate that around 70 percent of the sayings of Jesus represent some sort of wisdom utterance such as an aphorism, riddle, or parable. While the gospels portray Jesus as speaking in parables (one scholar counted 247 in the synoptic gospels), they should not be seen as mere illustrations of Jesus' preaching; they were, in fact, his primary vehicle of proclamation. Their distinctive connection to Jesus' ministry is borne out by the fact that other than in the gospels, the term "parable" appears nowhere else in the New Testament except in Hebrews 9:9 and 11:19.

We need to distinguish between proverbs, which are universally acceptable forms of communication, and aphorisms, which are enigmatic and innovative in nature. Whereas proverbs are associated with traditional wisdom, aphorisms are associated with counter-order wisdom. Jesus, like Qoheleth (the author of the Old Testament book Ecclesiastes), represents the latter, for there is little in the Jesus tradition that is purely proverbial. Surprisingly, many major themes of proverbial wisdom are absent from the teachings of Jesus. For example, none of his proverbs urge the seeking of wisdom, nor does he declare that the fear of the Lord is the beginning of wisdom. Jesus utters no proverbs or sayings commending hard work, nor does he offer conventional patriarchal wisdom about women such as found in Proverbs, or much less in the misogynist evaluation in Sirach 25:24.

Jesus not only countered the wisdom of the world, he used a controversial technique: the influence of the poor and marginal. While others sought the aid of the wealthy and the powerful, Jesus pronounced blessing on the "meek," the "merciful," the "poor in spirit," and even on the persecuted. Jesus' aphorisms are said to represent "wisdom from below," for they regularly challenge prevailing assumptions, giving voice to the poor and marginalized rather than to the privileged classes. Numerous sayings illustrate the parameters of the possible implied in God's new social order. For example, we think of the aphorism, "But many who are first will be last, and the last will be first" (Mark 10:31), or the riddle, "For those who want to save their life will lose it, and those who lose their life for my sake . . . will save it" (Mark 8:35). Moreover, we notice the absurdity in the aphorism, "It is easier for a camel to go through the eye of a needle than for someone who is rich to enter the kingdom of God" (Mark 10:25). The saying, "The sabbath was made for humankind, and not humankind for the sabbath" (Mark 2:27), suggests that Jesus was appealing to creation theology, which is characteristic of Jewish wisdom thought. However, he turned his appeal into an aphorism of counter-order in that he stood on his own authority in making a pronouncement that challenged the Mosaic/Levitical cultic tradition. In the statement about new wine and fresh wineskins ("no one puts new wine into old wineskins; otherwise, the wine will burst the skins, and the wine is lost, and so are the skins; but one puts new wine into fresh wineskins," Mark 2:22), Jesus points to his own ministry and mission as representing the coming of a new order.[1]

The study of Jewish wisdom literature indicates that parables were not characteristic of the canonical sages. Rather, they seem to have been a prophetic phenomenon, or at least prophetic adaptations of a wisdom form of utterance (see, for example, the court prophet Nathan's parable of condemnation of King David in 2 Samuel 12:1-4, or the allegorical riddle in Ezekiel 17:3-10). In Sirach we note a new development or understanding of the sage's role, the claim to be inspired as were the prophets: "I will again pour out teaching like prophecy" (24:33).[2] Similarly, in Wisdom 7:27 the sage informs his audience that when the spirit of wisdom passes into people's souls, she makes them "friends of God and prophets." Here the sage is seen as the one who delivers the prophetic word. Like these predecessors, Jesus

---

1. Though these citations are from Mark, they appear in Matthew and Luke as well.

2. This statement is unexpected, given the common Jewish belief that prophecy had ceased during the Restoration Period, following the classical prophets.

The Nature of Jesus' Teaching

seems to have viewed himself as a Jewish prophetic sage, appropriating various traditions in his role as teacher.

Matthew's gospel, written during the eighth decade of the first century, some ten years after the cataclysmic destruction of Jerusalem and the temple by the Romans in 70 CE, provides a significant understanding of Jesus not only as teacher but as master teacher, and provides textual support for a training school for Jewish Christian scribes. Indeed, throughout this gospel one finds an emphasis on pedagogy not found in the other gospels. For example, the end of the Sermon on the Mount makes clear that the first evangelist (the author of Matthew's gospel) wished to distinguish between Jesus the sage, who teaches as one who has independent authority, and "their scribes" (7:29), that is, Jewish teachers. In summary passages of Jesus' ministry, Matthew cites "teaching" ahead of preaching and healing as the chief task of Jesus (4:23; 9:35; and 11:1). This is significant when one notes that in Matthew's Markan source (Mark 1:39) there is no mention of teaching and no parallel to Matthew 9:35. In the Lukan parallel to Matthew 11:1, instead of "teach," one reads "after Jesus had finished all his sayings." When one examines the style of Jesus' teaching in Matthew, wisdom language predominates, for here Jesus offers beatitudes, aphorisms, parables, and wisdom discourses. In short, Matthew portrays Jesus as a Jewish sage. In 26:18 Jesus refers to himself as "The Teacher"; the assumption is that the reading audience knows who "the Teacher" is, and that those who hear are disciples.

Many scholars suggest that the statement in Matthew 13:52 provides a clue to how the evangelist saw himself: "Therefore every scribe who has been trained for the kingdom of heaven is like the master of a household who brings out of his treasure what is new and what is old." This uniquely Matthean saying indicates as much about the audience for whom this gospel was intended as it does about the author. The evangelist is one scribe showing other scribes the proper content and form of their teaching before they are sent out to make further disciples chiefly by teaching (see 28:19–20). Whereas Mark views the disciples as hardheaded and obtuse, not understanding the parables of Jesus, Matthew's inner circle of disciples understands even the more enigmatic wisdom teachings of Jesus (13:51).

Several additional passages reveal Matthew's purposes and aims in producing this gospel. In Matthew 16:17–19, Peter is given the keys of the kingdom, explained as binding and loosing (in 18:18 the entire church is given this authority). One way to interpret this imagery is as referring to the teaching authority of the church, in this case, the commissioning of scribes with authority to teach, transmit, and interpret the Jesus tradition. Matthew 10:24–25a, the first commissioning scene in Matthew's gospel, states that a disciple is not to be above "*the* teacher," but rather is called to be *like* his teacher. This passage, unique to Matthew, prepares readers for the culminating scene in 28:18–20, where the evangelist summarizes various wisdom and pedagogical themes, particularly obeying commandments and teaching others, two tasks of disciples.

Thus at crucial junctures in Matthew's gospel—at the end of the first discourse (7:28–29); at the first commissioning of the disciples (10:24); at Caesarea Philippi, when Peter is granted the keys (16:19); at the close of the chapter on parables (13:52); and at the Great Commission that ends the book (28:19–20)—Jesus is portrayed as Teacher and the disciples as teacher-scribes.

At the conclusion of the Sermon on the Mount we find these remarkable words: "the crowds were astonished at his teaching, for he taught them as one having authority, and not as their scribes" (Matt 7:28–29). A central feature of Jesus' preaching and teaching was the degree of authority with which he spoke. Rabbis (scribes), as teachers of Torah, derived authority from scripture. The prevailing approach of Jesus' day, used by rabbis, was to quote previous rabbis. Scribes never spoke solely on their own authority, for they derived their authority ultimately from Moses, whom they viewed as mediator of God's law.

Earlier in the Sermon, in the antithetical sayings of Matthew 5:21–48, Jesus quoted traditional Jewish legal statements, believed to be based upon the Torah of Moses ("you have heard that it was said"), only to intensify or surpass their original meaning ("but I say to you"). Unlike the scribes of his day, Jesus appealed to his own authority. This approach embodied a claim that rivaled and surpassed that of Moses. Scribes may have challenged one another in debate, but Jesus challenged the Law of Moses. To this, there is no Jewish parallel.

How are we to explain the authoritative nature of Jesus' teaching? While we cannot provide a final answer, the only reasonable explanation must be based on Jesus' claim of an immediate relationship to God, in the strict sense of being unmediated. When Jesus spoke of God as "Father," this intimacy was not theoretical but personal in nature: Jesus *knew* God as Father. In addition, Jesus was able to communicate to others the assurance of what he taught. Building on this important foundation, he was able to translate religious experience into transformational action, into *doing*, and not simply into hearing (Matt 7:24–27).

For Jesus, the essence of God's will is practical, meaning it is to be manifested both privately and publicly (Matt 22:36–40). The Christian ethic, then, is based on sincerity (on inward attitudes and motivation, Matt 6:1–4), but it flows forth into social responsibility, as demonstrated in "the Golden Rule": "In everything do to others as you would have them do to you; for this is the law and the prophets" (Matt 7:12).

The important element in the ministry of Jesus is that he not only lived according to the highest standards, but that he inspired others to follow his example.

Questions for Discussion and Reflection

Having read chapter 6, answer the following questions, writing your answers in a journal. If you are in a group study, be prepared to share your answers with those in the group.

1. In your estimation, does the fact that Jesus grew up in obscurity and anonymity, a peasant seemingly without religious credentials or formal training, add or detract from his preaching and teaching authority? Explain your answer.

2. If Jesus were to appear today lacking requisite credentials, would anyone pay him much attention?

3. In your estimation, what about Jesus' teaching qualifies him as a master teacher?

4. In your estimation, was Jesus a unifier or a divider, a comforter or a disturber? In your assessment, what role do Jesus' parables play in his mission?

5. In your understanding of the Jewish wisdom literature, explain the distinction between "conventional wisdom" and "counter-order wisdom" and how, in his teaching and way of life, Jesus modeled the latter.

6. Explain the similarities and differences between proverbs and parables.

7. In your estimation, why did Jesus choose to convey "Truth" through parables?

8. If parables were central to Jesus' teaching and preaching, why are parables rarely if ever used outside the gospels in the ongoing literary tradition contained within the New Testament?
9. Explain the distinction between Jesus as traditional sage and as prophetic sage.
10. If Jesus can be characterized as a prophetic sage, why did he never resort to the prophetic formula, "Thus says the Lord"?
11. After reading this chapter, what did you learn about the purpose and setting of Mathew's gospel and of its portrayal of Jesus as sage?

7

God's New Reality

IN THE BIBLE, TEACHING concerning salvation and the afterlife is very much a part of its eschatological perspective. Eschatology is the study of final things, including the resurrection of the dead, the Last Judgment, the defeat of evil, the end of this world, and the creation of a new one. A fully formed eschatology with all of these features emerged only late in the development of biblical traditions.

The classic prophets of Israel were mostly concerned with the events of history, speaking boldly and without compromise against current disobedience and disbelief within the social, religious, and political establishment. Biblical prophets rarely, if ever, made open predictions about the future, and when they did so, the predictions were linked to their role as social critics, which focused on the consequences for unrepentance. The prophet's futuristic role was associated primarily with the certainty of the coming of the Lord, a coming to make things right through judgment and reward.

Toward the end of the sixth century BCE, after the Jews returned from the Babylonian captivity, they held on to the prophetic hopes and visions, longing for a time when they could function once again under theocratic ideals. During the postexilic period, the prophetic expectation expanded to include messianic hope, longing for the arrival of God's kingdom. But the kingdom of God did not materialize, and messianic hope had to be deferred.

As time went on, some persecuted members of the Jewish community became pessimistic about an earthly kingdom of God and looked for salvation from above through direct intervention from God. This led to the development of apocalyptic eschatology, found in postexilic passages added to the book of Isaiah dubbed the Isaianic apocalypse (Isaiah 24–27) and Third Isaiah (Isaiah 56–66). These passages speculate about end-time events, including the Lord's arrival as king on Mount Zion, the judgment of the nations accompanied by heavenly portents, the abolition of death, the resurrection of the dead, the destruction of Leviathan (the chaos monster), and the creation of a new heaven and a new earth.

Like the prophets, apocalyptists expected an end followed by a new era of God's saving activity. But the apocalyptists saw the end as complete and final. The judgment would be not only on Israel but on all nations. This judgment would include not only their earthly foes but the cosmic forces of evil as well.

Many of these elements appear in the New Testament, for early Christianity inherited its eschatological framework from Judaism. To understand Jesus and the gospels, scholars suggest three eschatological perspectives: (1) "consistent eschatology," meaning that Jesus' eschatological teachings as presented in the gospels refer only to what will happen at the end of the world; (2) "realized eschatology," meaning that Jesus understood the anticipated kingdom of God to have arrived with himself; and (3) "inaugurated eschatology," meaning that Jesus brought the dawning of the awaited kingdom. This latter view finds some aspects of God's reign to be present in Jesus, but other elements of the kingdom would not appear until the very end. It is clear from passages such as the Synoptic Apocalypse (see Mark 13; Matt 24–25; and Luke 21), where signs of the end are given, that Jesus believed the fullness of the kingdom would arrive shortly, probably within his generation (see Mark 13:30).

For the writers of the New Testament, Jesus' followers are situated between the inauguration of the kingdom of God and its consummation. In the meantime, they are to be busy preaching the gospel, doing good works, and modeling exemplary lives.

Jesus and the Presence of the Kingdom

The dominant theme in the preaching of Jesus—indeed the center of his mission and message—is the coming of the kingdom of God. While the phrase "kingdom of God" is rare in contemporary Jewish writings, it is widely regarded as one of the most distinctive aspects of the preaching of Jesus. Because almost everywhere in the Old Testament the idea of the kingdom is related to the people of Israel and the rule of the house of David

God's New Reality

in Jerusalem, Jesus was at pains to divest his teaching of this former understanding of the nature of the kingdom. What Jesus proclaimed was the immediate sovereignty of God, who would take control of the destinies of all humans, restore humanity to what God had intended it to be, and overthrow the evil powers that had led astray human beings from their proper destiny.[1]

In Mark's gospel, Jesus' first act upon returning from his sojourn in the wilderness is to proclaim the coming of the kingdom (1:15). Here Jesus is picking up where Second Isaiah left off half a millennium earlier. Isaiah had envisioned a day when God would finally bring justice to the world, when the long-suffering faithful could rejoice at the end of oppression. Jesus shared Isaiah's anticipation but was more specific about when this time would come: "Truly I tell you, there are some standing here who will not taste death until they see that the kingdom of God has come with power" (Mark 9:1). His audience was to repent and "believe in the good news."

Whatever Jesus envisioned in his proclamation about the kingdom, it was going to be on earth. Despite Matthew's preference for the expression, "kingdom of heaven," it is clear that the concept, as Jesus used it, refers to the destiny of good people on a new, improved earth. It has nothing to do with the souls of dead people ascending to heaven.

In New Testament teaching the coming of the kingdom is always dependent on divine initiative, never on human achievement. Humans may enter the kingdom; they may proclaim it and inherit it (Matt 25:34; 7:21), but they can neither earn it nor bring it forth. Because the word "kingdom" suggests a geographical region or realm, which is misleading in this context, scholars prefer the term "kingship" or "kingly rule of God."

The term "kingdom" is complex and paradoxical at its core. In the synoptic gospels, the paradoxical nature of the kingdom is manifested in several ways: (a) it is present (Matt 12:28; Luke 17:21), yet not fully present (Matt 8:29; 13:30); (b) it is a gift (Matt 25:34; Luke 12:32), yet it also involves human effort (Matt 6:33; Luke 12:31); (c) it is an internal reality (Luke 17:20–21), yet it has external implications for the world (Matt 6:10). Scholars are particularly interested in the first of these, for it addresses the tension between the present time and the future, the "already" and the "not yet." In that regard, they have introduced the term "inaugurated

---

1. Because of the negativity many people today associate with the term "kingdom," Brian McLaren offers six metaphors that, taken together, help describe the meaning of the phrase "kingdom of God" for us today: (1) the dream of God, (2) the revolution of God, (3) the mission of God, (4) the party of God, (5) the network of God, and (6) the dance of God. *Secret Message of Jesus*, 138–48.

eschatology" to refer to the relation of the present inauguration and the future fulfillment of the kingdom.

There is a present element in the New Testament concept of the kingdom, particularly in the teaching of Jesus, which is colored by a sense of intense urgency. God has already taken the initiative; humans are challenged to recognize the reality of the present situation and to make such decisions as will qualify them to become citizens of the kingdom. The signs of the presence of the kingdom are already present in the ministry of Jesus. When John the Baptist questions the mission of Jesus and asks for signs, he is given clear evidence: "the blind receive their sight, the lame walk, the lepers are cleansed, the deaf hear, the dead are raised, and the poor have good news brought to them" (Matt 11:5). All these are signs that the power of the kingdom is presently at work. Those who refuse to recognize that the power evident in Jesus is a power from God are told: "if it is by the finger of God that I cast out the demons, then the kingdom of God has come to you" (Luke 11:20). When one person, for a period of some thirty-five years, lives in total dependence upon God, with a unique understanding of God's will and in unconditional surrender to it, the kingdom is already present. As Jesus tells the Pharisees in answer to their question about when the kingdom was coming: "the kingdom of God is among you" (Luke 17:21).

According to the New Testament, Christians are kind of hybrid creatures who live in two dimensions. They are citizens of the present age while at the same time living under the dominion of Christ's kingdom. As Paul put it somewhat paradoxically, Christians live "in the flesh" (human nature) and also "in the Spirit" (the new dimension introduced by Christ). Awareness of this dual citizenship led early Christians to say that they were "strangers" in the historical era on earth (Heb 11:13).

Ever since the New Testament period, Christianity has had to steer between two dangers: the temptation (1) to withdraw from society on the assumption that Christ's kingdom is not of this world (John 18:36), and (2) to make a too easy identification of the kingdom with something in this world, such as the institutional church or the ideal human society. However, the essential message of the New Testament is this: The kingdom is not of this world, yet it has been manifest in this world through the life, death, and resurrection of Christ. Although God's kingdom is a higher order than any political reality or human ideal of the present age, it has influenced and penetrated the kingdoms of this world—not as a tangent touches a circle but as a vertical line intersects a horizontal plane. The task of the church is to bear witness to this "vertical dimension" of history and, in so doing, to seek to leaven and redeem society in the name of Christ. This attitude toward society is not one of "detachment" but of "transfiguration," involving a rhythm of withdrawal and return through worship and action, faith and good works.

The tension between the "already" and the "not yet" nature of the kingdom is evident also in Paul's eschatology. At several points Paul emphasizes that the coming of Jesus inaugurates a new era or "age," which he designates a "new creation" (2 Cor 5:17). While the presence of this new age can already be experienced, for Paul the ultimate transformation of the world is yet to come. Viewing the resurrection of Jesus as eschatological event, for it confirms that the "new age" is truly present, Paul also looks ahead to the future coming of Jesus Christ in judgment at the end of time. Another theme of Paul's eschatology is the coming of the Holy Spirit. This theme, which builds on a long-standing aspect of Jewish expectation, sees the gift of the Spirit as a confirmation that the new age has dawned in Christ. One of the most significant aspects of Paul's thought is his interpretation of the gift of the Spirit to believers as a "guarantee" or "first installment" of ultimate salvation (2 Cor 1:22; 5:5).

Realized Eschatology

There are a great many problems on planet earth these days, ecological, social, political, and economic, and a common Christian response is to long for Christ's return to judge the earth and take believers to heaven. Non-believers often associate such hope with wish-fulfillment, calling it "pie in the sky by and by." Is Christianity escapist? Are its solutions to world problems futuristic, impractical, and unrealistic? For the answer, people often turn to the doctrine of eschatology, an aspect of theology that deals with the end-times and the "*eschaton*," a Greek word meaning "the end of history" or "the final event."

If eschatology is the study of "final things," it would be easy to believe that God's promises of renewal and redemption, whether of nature or of humanity, will occur at the end of time, when the new heaven and the new earth are revealed. Such thinking, however, is not biblical. Even though the final life in all its fullness has not yet arrived, a life with God is possible in the present. One aspect of eschatology that is often ignored or overlooked is known as "realized eschatology," a view associated with the British biblical scholar C. H. Dodd. This outlook speaks of final things as being with us now. A life with God is possible in the present, even though that final life in all its fullness has not yet arrived.

Scholars speak of a tension in the New Testament between "the already and the not yet," meaning that God's long-awaited eschatological transformation of reality, including the coming of the kingdom of God and the judgment of evil and reward of faith (eternal life), is underway in the present, initiated by Jesus' coming into the world and later in the coming of the Holy Spirit.

Proponents of "realized eschatology" note that according to the gospels, Jesus began his ministry by announcing that the time had come for God to begin God's reign on earth, and that the first Christians understood this was happening in Jesus' own person and work. The Good News of the gospel was not that the kingdom was about to be realized on earth, but that the kingdom had actually arrived, and that its power was already present: "For, in fact, the kingdom of God is among [or within] you" (Luke 17:21).

According to Mark's gospel, the preaching ministry of Jesus was eschatological in nature, summarized by the New Revised Standard Version as: "The time is fulfilled, and the kingdom of God *has come near*" (Mark 1:15). Earlier versions, including the King James and the Revised Standard Version, translate the Greek word rendered "has come near" differently: "the kingdom of God *is at hand*." To say that the kingdom "has come near," as later versions correctly indicate, means that God's reign is uniquely available in Christ. This does not mean, however, that it is fully here, as C. H. Dodd maintained, arguing for the translation "the kingdom of God *has come*," or that the kingdom was only available in the first century, or in Palestine, Israel, or in any other specific territory on earth.

The phrase "kingdom of God," a concept found in the Lord's Prayer ("Thy kingdom come, Thy will be done, on earth as it is in heaven") and throughout the gospels, is often misunderstood as referring to an earthly institution such as the church, or to a geographical territory or state such as the Vatican, but as the prayer tells us, using a traditional Hebrew literary style known as "synonymous parallelism," the kingdom of God is present on earth wherever and whenever God's will is as fully done as it is in heaven. That is to say, to do the will of God and to be in the kingdom are one and the same thing. Hence it might be better to speak of the "rule" or "reign" of God rather than the "kingdom" of God. While Jesus' Jewish audience understood God's coming rule in terms of material prosperity, political power, and national greatness, that is not what Jesus intended. When Jesus is quoted as saying to Pilate, "My kingdom is not from (of) this world" (John 18:36), Jesus meant that his rule was unlike other worldly kingdoms, political, material, or national in nature. On the positive side, equating the "kingdom of God" with the "will of God" indicates the universality of God's rule. There are no racial, social, or gender distinctions in God's rule, no favored peoples or nations.

Furthermore, this emphasis has powerful ethical implications. The notion of God's rule on earth challenges all attachments to centers of value and power that serve egocentric impulses. Divine primacy relativizes all idolatries—including the gods of nation, self, class, family, race, gender, institution, success, money, sexuality, and even religion—to the status of proximal goods. Any claim of ultimacy for them or by them must be avoided or relinquished. This means that social distinctions by which humans define themselves have only relative value and therefore are not indicative of ultimate value or worth.[2]

To pray "Thy kingdom come" is not to imply, however, that God's rule is not here, for God's kingdom is always present in seed form, always near and growing. That is why for Jesus the growth of the mustard seed, the smallest of seeds, into a tree symbolized the kingdom (Matt 13:31–32). Our actions can delay the kingdom and hinder its power, but the kingdom will be near until its consummation, for it is based on God's promise of ongoing renewal and transformation.

In the New Testament, the gospel of John maintains a delicate eschatological balance between "the already and the not yet." Passages such as John 3:17–21, 31–36, and 6:47 exemplify realized eschatology. The very presence of Jesus in the world confronts the world with a decision, to believe or not to believe, and making that decision is the moment of judgment. John 3:18 explains that this judgment is underway in the present, initiated by Jesus' coming into the world (see 3:36). If one's life is characterized by transformative belief, so that one's deeds are "done in God" (John 3:21), then one *already* has eternal life (3:36); if one does not believe, one is *already* condemned. John's gospel does include traditional understandings of eschatology and the final judgment (5:28–29; 12:48), but judgment and eternal life as present realities are at the theological heart of the Fourth Gospel.

As John affirmed eternal life as already present for the followers of Jesus, he also believed in realized wrath, that God's wrath is already present

---

2. Fowler, *Stages of Faith*, 205.

for those who reject and disobey God. For John, there are always moral consequences to one's actions, both sooner and later.

"Eternal life," the term John uses instead of "the kingdom of God," is not something believers possess only after death. It begins as soon as one places trust in Jesus as God's Son. Contemporary Christians have become so used to associating eternal life with going to heaven that the idea of realized eschatology, which views the future as somehow present now, seems perplexing.

The notion of "eternal life," like the "kingdom of God," is paradoxical at its core. Like the kingdom, eternal life is already present, yet not fully so. This becomes clearer when we understand that "eternal life" has as much to do with the quality and direction of life as with the length of one's existence. A better term might be "everlasting life," meaning a life that begins for believers in this lifetime but continues on forever.

We live in a time of deep division, in which mind is at odds with body, and spirituality with matter. We need a way out of the dualistic attitudes that permeate our thinking, permeable boundaries between polarities such as good and evil, God and Satan, light and darkness, spirit and flesh, eternal life and eternal death, belief and disbelief, truth and falsehood, heaven and hell, heaven and earth. Dualism claims independent reality for each polarity, whereas the truth is that the negative item in the pair derives somehow from its opposite. As cold is the absence of heat, so evil is the absence of good, and so forth.

As the book of Revelation makes clear, soft boundaries exist between spatial and temporal planes and even between good and evil. Evil contrasts with good, but evil is not of a fundamentally different order from good. Even God and Satan, the epitome of good and evil respectively, are not separated by hard, impervious boundaries, for in the Bible the "demonic" plane derives from the heavenly, divine plane. While boundaries do exist between heaven and earth, future and present, deity and humanity, and good and evil, there is dynamism to boundaries. Boundaries do not fix limits beyond which it is impossible to pass. Rather they locate the place where transformations occur, allowing a flow across planes, eras, social categories, and moral values.

In the Bible, "heaven" is the starting point for all revelation. We should not, however, restrict "heaven" to the spiritual dimension of reality, for it represents more than that. In the book of Revelation, what John sees in heaven is not simply divine perspective. "Heaven" represents what is right and good and proper. When Jesus tells his followers to pray, "Your kingdom come . . . on earth as it is in heaven" (Matt. 6:10), he understands "heaven" not as a future destination for humans but as God's dimension of everyday reality. Heaven is in charge; heaven takes the lead; heaven represents what ought to be happening on earth now.

In the Bible, to live with agape love now is to live out of the resources of the future, and when Christians live that way, they demonstrate not only the reality of eternal life, but the fact that it is available in the present. No one understood that better than Elizabeth Barrett Browning, who penned these memorable words:

> Earth's crammed with heaven,
> And every common bush afire with God;
> And he who sees it takes off his shoes—
> The rest sit round it and pluck blackberries.[3]

No one can live a good life alone, and no one can be moral in isolation. Learning and sustaining the virtues that transform a person who has the gifts of faith, hope, and love into a person with a full moral life require self-knowledge and self-disciple. The tasks are sometimes lonely, but they are not accomplished alone. We live our faith in a community with others, both in the community of faith that is the church and in the wider civic community. One of the most persistent questions of our time is whether these communities in which we live are the sorts of places that can support us in the effort to live a good life.

Can our churches teach us virtue? What should we make of the tensions, conflicts, and divisions among Christians that often seem to bring out the worst in them, rather than enable them to live at their best? Can we expect assistance in living virtuously from the businesses, schools, and governments around us, or must we actively resist the values they teach in order to live a good life?

One thing is certain; the biblical emphasis on renewal is always "now": "*Now* is the acceptable time; now is the day of salvation" (2 Cor 6:2), and "*Today*, if you hear his voice, do not harden your hearts" (Heb 4:7). Those who expect apocalyptic solutions, whether through divine judgment at the end of history or via Christ's return, may wait indefinitely. If renewal is to occur, it must occur now. Those who read the Bible with wisdom eyes come to see that the kingdom, like Christ's second coming, is an ever-recurring

---

3. *Aurora Leigh*, Book VII, Line 820.

reality. Just as the kingdom is always breaking into our lives, so Christ is forever entering our consciousness, ever transforming our living, thinking, and being.

Our task in the present, according to Jesus, is to ask, search, and knock: "Ask, and it will be given you; search, and you will find; knock, and the door will be opened for you. For everyone who asks receives, and everyone who searches find, and for everyone who knocks, the door will be opened" (Matt 7:7–8). The emphasis here is active and present: these are things we need to be doing now. And if we strive first for the kingdom of God and its righteousness, all good things will be given to us as well (Matt 6:33).

As Paul indicates, God is a promissory God, fulfilling all promises in Christ (2 Cor 1:20) and through the Holy Spirit, given as a guarantee of divine faithfulness (2 Cor 5:5). God renews both cosmos and humanity by the Spirit, indwelling believers, inspiring their mission, and dispensing gifts freely by grace. And the message of scripture is clear: this God loves us unconditionally.

To take eschatology seriously is to see that the hoped-for present comes to us out of the future. Receiving the present from God's future frees us from the shackles of the past. Seen in the light of biblical hope, the human vocation is to live in anticipation of the ever-coming rule of God, leaning into God's promised future for us and for all being. To live this way is to be part of the reconciling, redeeming, and restoring work that goes on wherever the kingdom of God is breaking in.

According to the Bible, there is a moral force in the universe. Ultimately injustice will be defeated. As biblical prophets indicate, one cannot get away with injustice. God listens to the voice of the weak and the marginalized, and no individual, institution, or society that supports oppression is safe, whether secular or religious. As prophets know, challenging injustice produces hope, particularly hope for change on this earth. In that spirit, listen anew to the words Jesus taught his disciples to pray: "Your kingdom come, Your will be done, *on earth* as it is in heaven" (Matt 6:10).

As we have seen, hope rooted in promise is related to change, not only for individuals but also for society. John of Patmos, visualizing a "new heaven and a new earth" (Rev 21:1), quotes God as saying: "See, I am making all things new" (Rev 21:5). When Jesus speaks of faith moving mountains (Mark 11:23), such mountains surely include problems that plague us today, evils such as racism, sexism, terrorism, militarism, jingoism, materialism, xenophobia, pollution, poverty, domestic violence, and addictive behavior.

As we sing in church: "Let there be peace on earth, and let it begin with me." When will this change happen? If it doesn't begin now, with us, it may not happen at all. What scourge will your faith help eliminate from our planet?

Christians, empowered by God's Spirit, are to live positively, as Jesus did, out of the resources of the kingdom, rather than negatively, out of the resources of the moment. As citizens of God's kingdom, Christians are to live as the salt of the earth and the light of the world (Matt 5:13–16), rather than suspiciously, fearfully, and impotently.

If faith, hope, and love exist, basic to morality yet beyond human invention, then I submit they come as gifts from a benevolent deity. If God is Lover, Giver, and Creator, then we live in a loving, moral universe, with grace as its cornerstone. Our responsibility, then, is to live graciously on planet earth, empowered by the resources of God, whose image we bear.

According to the gospels, Jesus began his ministry by announcing that the time had come for God to begin God's reign on earth. The Good News of the gospel was not that God's kingdom was about to be realized on earth, but rather that the kingdom had actually arrived, and that its power was already present. Indeed, eternal life, the term John's gospel uses instead of "the kingdom of God," is already present, though not fully so. When Jesus speaks of faith moving mountains, such mountains include the problems that plague us today. Christian hope is not "pie in the sky by and by," but radical power to tackle head-on today's problems and to defeat them. To live with agape love now is to live out of the resources of the future, and when Christians live like that, they demonstrate not only the reality of eternal life, but the fact that it is available in the present.

The Second Coming of Christ and the End of History

The world as we know it will end; that is a scientific fact. However, if someone tells you they know when history will end or how it will end, or provides details concerning the second coming of Christ, pay no attention, for such knowledge is not given to mortals.

In the Bible, much of the language about the future is couched in eschatological or apocalyptic imagery. It flows from the hopes and fears of first-century believers living under oppressive Roman rule. Such imagery is imaginative and speculative; it is not predictive, and should not be taken literally.

Throughout history and in our time as well there have been bold and detailed predictions about the end time, and all have proven wrong. Scripture warns us about false prophets and teachers (see Matt 24:11–13) and exhorts every generation to focus on the present rather than on the unknown future. In the week before his crucifixion, Jesus cautioned his disciples not to speculate about situations of uncertainty: "But about that day and hour no one knows, neither the angels of heaven, nor the Son, but only the Father" (Matt 24:36). Earlier, when teaching about prayer, Jesus had exhorted his disciples to focus on earthly realities while praying for daily needs (see the Lord's Prayer in Matt 6:10–11).

In the book of Acts, the resurrected Jesus counters the disciples' request for a timetable of end-time events with timely advice: "It is not for you to know such things. Your goal is to be faithful with the opportunities at hand. For this task you will be empowered by God's Holy Spirit" (Acts 1:7–8 paraphrased). The apostle Paul encourages his readers with similar advice: "Finally, beloved, whatever is true, whatever is honorable, whatever is just, whatever is pure, whatever is pleasing, whatever is commendable . . . , think about these things. Keep on doing the things that you have learned and received and heard and seen" (Phil 4:8–9).

We hear much nowadays in the media about "the rapture of believers to heaven" before the great tribulation on earth. We should not succumb to such speculation, for the word "rapture" is not biblical, and the concept represents a misinterpretation of scripture. While scripture tells us to await the coming of Christ, it is more helpful to think of Christ's return as an ongoing reality that empowers us in the present, rather than as a singular event awaited in the future. In some passages of the Bible, the emphasis is on the ongoing coming of Christ into the lives of believers, bringing to every generation the promise of God's power and presence. When, in John's gospel, the resurrected Jesus bestowed the Holy Spirit on the disciples (see John 20:22), Jesus unleashed resurrection power on present and future followers. With that empowerment, the focus shifted from the old to the new, from the anticipated future to the proleptic present. The marching orders are clear: "As the Father has sent me, so I send you." For those in Christ, for those in the Spirit, the future is now (see Paul's realized eschatology in 2 Cor 5:17). Together, we are God's anticipated future!

The book of Revelation sets the record straight. Christians are not raptured to heaven to escape the sufferings of earth. The author knows nothing of a "rapture" of believers to escape earthly tribulation. Rather, Christians are to conquer on earth through suffering and death, as Jesus did. The church's experience of being called by God is not to escape from this earth. Christians are not spared trials and tribulations, but rather experience God's presence and care *through* life's struggles. At the end of Revelation, humans are not translated to a celestial realm, for God dwells on earth; and where God is, there is heaven. Instead of envisioning the followers of Christ as "raptured" from earth, it is more helpful to think of them as the ones who are "left behind," that is, who are called to embody God's kingdom and its values on earth. Contrary to ideas about the "rapture" of the church from earth at the second coming of Christ, there is no such "rapture" in Revelation. Instead, it is God who is "raptured" to earth to live with us.

The Bible tells us not to worry about the unknown future, for it is secure in God's hands. Christians need not live by fear, but rather by faith in the certainty of God's unconditional love. If someone fears punishment because he or she has broken God's commandments, God's remedy is clear. It appears all throughout scripture, but perhaps most clearly in three passages:

1. In John 3:16 we learn that the "world" (in John's gospel this is a term not simply for the created order but for the realm of doubt and disbelief) is the object of God's love. Unlike human love, God's love is not possessive or selective. God does not simply love those who are converts, or who are "born again," or who love God in return. Rather, in Christ God so loved the sinful world that God gave the very best: Godself. If people act in evil and hurtful ways because they belong to the world and its values, how can such evil be overcome? John's answer sounds simple, but it represents what Christian theologian Dietrich Bonhoeffer termed "costly grace": by walking in the light, a form of discipleship described as living life abundantly (John 10:10). While it sounds simple, the journey from darkness to light requires continuous transformation of the self, a process John entrusts to the Holy Spirit.

2. In 1 John 4:18 we learn that "there is no fear in love, but perfect love casts out fear." God's remedy for fear, guilt, and wrongdoing is not punishment or self-recrimination but love: love for God and love for others. Surprisingly, in such loving, the starting point is not the former but the latter. By loving family members, neighbors, and those in need here on earth, we demonstrate our love for God: "If we love one another, God lives in us, and his love is perfected in us" (1 John 4:12).

3. In James 1:27 we learn that practical love, not mystical or heroic love, defines true religion: "Religion that is pure and undefiled . . . is this: to care for orphans and widows in their distress, and to keep oneself unstained by the [self-centered, unbelieving] world."

Questions For Discussion and Reflection

Having read chapter 7, answer the following questions, writing your answers in a journal. If you are in a group study, be prepared to share your answers with those in the group.

1. Explain how early Christianity inherited its eschatological perspective from Judaism.
2. Explain the differences between "consistent," "realized," and "inaugurated" eschatology. In your estimation, which view best represents the perspective of the historical Jesus? Explain your answer.
3. In a sentence or two define what is meant by "the kingdom of God."
4. Evaluate the perspective called "realized eschatology," including the merits and disadvantages of holding such a view.
5. Should John's gospel's perspective of "realized eschatology" be viewed as a peculiarity of that gospel, or should John's emphasis on "the already" nature of the kingdom be determinative for Christian thinking and living?
6. Should we think of "heaven" primarily as a place of future reward or primarily as "God's dimension of everyday reality," as the text suggests? What difference might these alternative ways of thinking about "heaven" have on our lifestyle?
7. In your estimation, what does Elizabeth Barrett Browning mean in her poem when she writes: "he who sees it takes off his shoes"? What is she suggesting by the words, "The rest sit round it and pluck blackberries"?
8. When Jesus spoke of faith moving mountains (Mark 11:23), which social "mountain" will your faith help to eliminate from our planet?
9. Do you agree that too many Christians seek Christ's return (known popularly as "the rapture" of believers to heaven) as the solution to

the world's problems? Does Paul's advice to believers in his day "living in idleness" (that is, sitting and waiting for Christ's return; see 2 Thess 3:6–15) apply to the current mindset of those who wait for "the rapture" as a solution to the world's evil?

10. In your estimation, how does agape love, exhibited through the lives of selfless and courageous believers, embody God's kingdom on earth?

8

Jesus and Jewish Eschatology

DURING THE INTERTESTAMENTAL PERIOD, when the culture and religion of the Jews were seriously threatened by the rise of Hellenism, a new phase of prophetic activity, known as apocalypticism, emerged. Some of its literary and theological characteristics are already perceptible in Ezekiel, Isaiah 56–66, and Zechariah 1–8. Joel 1–3 and Zechariah 9–14, in addition to Isaiah 24–27, are later examples of this category. However, the classic representation of this type of literature in the Old Testament canon is Daniel, written during the Maccabean crisis of 168–65 BCE.

While the distant future was not central to the prophets, it was not overlooked, for eschatology was basic to the prophetic message. Israel's prophets consistently looked beyond the present, in which God's purpose seemed to be temporarily opposed by Israel's rebellion, to a time when God would triumph over the forces of evil. Prophetic predictions of the triumph of God's purpose were expressed in phrases like "the Day of the Lord," "the Age to Come," and "the Kingdom of God." In their vision the consummation of history was to be a time of reckoning, when all rebellious powers would be judged and destroyed. It was also to be the beginning of a New Creation in which nature and human nature would be transformed. No longer would there be war, and even wild animals would be tame (Isa 65:17–25). The pictures of the messianic age remind us of the idyllic peace and harmony of the Garden of Eden prior to the expulsion. The prophets proclaimed that the Day was imminent, as near as the next moment of history.

The theme of apocalyptic literature, which flourished in the postexilic period, was, like that of prophecy, the nearness of the time when God would assert sovereignty over history and nature. It is characteristic of apocalyptic, however, that specific historical events receded into the background, and the contest between God and rebellious forces assumed a cosmic scale. Apocalyptic writers were dualistic in their view of history. They perceived two dominions (kingdoms) struggling for dominance. The kingdom of God stands opposed to the well-organized kingdom of Evil that is under the leadership of Satan. This is not a metaphysical dualism, however, rooted in ultimate reality or in the depths of divinity, for God's original creation was good. Rather, this is a postcreation dualism rooted in creaturely rebellion against God—rebellion that is evident not only in human sin but also in cosmic revolt by celestial beings. The conflict between the forces of God and the forces of evil was eventually expressed in terms of the myth of Satan, a heavenly being who revolted against God and set up a rival kingdom into which human beings are enticed. These two dominions may also be described as two "ages" or "worlds," that is, times of history. The present "age," in the apocalyptic view, is under the dominion of evil, and it will be succeeded by the "new age," when evil is overcome and all things are made new.

The End will be heralded by unusual "signs" and cataclysms in nature. On the Day of Judgment, God (or God's messianic agent) will destroy all powers of evil and will create a new heaven and a new earth. As we see in the book of Daniel, the purpose of apocalyptic writers was to encourage the faithful to remain steadfast in a perilous hour when allegiance to God was temporarily eclipsed by foreign tyranny or the victory of evil. The use of fantastic imagery in books like Ezekiel and Daniel clearly indicates that the language was intended to be imaginative. The heart of the apocalyptic message was the certainty that God's purpose could not be frustrated—a certainty that found expression in the nearness of the End. This is the only way that a new age of peace and justice can come: God must destroy the whole evil system.

As a first-century Palestinian Jew, Jesus belonged to a world where religion (theology) and politics went hand in hand. The theology was Jewish monotheism, a doctrine forged through centuries of subjugation and persecution, going back to the Babylonian exile (sixth century BCE). First-century Jews held their monotheism passionately. Theirs was not an abstract theory about the existence of one God. They believed that their God, Yahweh, was the only God, and that all others were idols. A corollary of monotheism was "election," the belief that the Jews had been chosen by this one God, making what happened to Israel of universal significance. Many Jews of Jesus' day believed that God was about to vindicate them, understanding this act as having global implications, as the means of divine judgment and/or mercy upon the rest of the world.

Ancient Jewish monotheists, believing in one God and in their status as God's elect people, while currently suffering oppression, also believed the present state of affairs to be temporary. Monotheism and election thus gave birth to eschatology, a perspective that views history as purposeful and therefore as moving toward a climactic resolution or restoration, at which time everything would be made right. First-century Jewish eschatology claimed that Yahweh would soon act within history to vindicate his people and to establish permanent justice and peace. This belief included the great promises of forgiveness articulated by biblical prophets such as Isaiah, Jeremiah, and Ezekiel. The exilic and post-exilic prophets spoke of a restoration still to be described, a liberation they described as a new exodus (see Isa 51:9–11; see also 43:2; 44:27).

In keeping with this understanding, it follows that Jesus of Nazareth might have viewed his mission as prophetic, announcing, like John the Baptist before him, God's coming kingdom. But Jesus, it seems, went beyond John's verbal role, embodying in his person and his ministry the presence of that kingdom. For Jesus, the all-encompassing rule of God was near, which when it came in its fullness, would restore Israel's role as "light to the nations" and challenge evil in all its manifestations, political, social, and economic. The coming kingdom of God was not a new sort of religion, a new moral code, or a new soteriology (a doctrine about how one might go to heaven after death). Nor was it a new sociological analysis, critique, or agenda. It was about Israel's story reaching its climax, about Israel's history moving toward its decisive moment.[1]

E. P. Sanders, in his classic text *Jesus and Judaism*, maintains that before the outbreak of the War of the Jews against Rome in 66 CE, "common Judaism" held the following hopes for the future: the restoration of the tribes of Israel; the conversion, destruction, or subjugation of the Gentiles; the renewal of Jerusalem, including a new or rebuilt temple; and the purification of God's people and their worship."[2] Whatever one makes of his idea of a common Judaism, surely the beliefs Sanders highlights were widespread among Jesus' contemporaries, as was apocalyptic eschatology in general.

1. Borg and Wright, *Meaning of Jesus*, 31–35.
2. Sanders, *Jesus and Judaism*, 279–303.

Jesus and Jewish Eschatology

According to Sanders, Jesus was an apocalyptic prophet standing in the tradition of Jewish restoration theology. He shared the beliefs common in Judaism, together with this prevailing understanding of Israel's story and hope. Having established the essential Jewishness of Jesus on this topic, Sanders finds primitive Christianity to be a movement in continuity with Jesus' hopes and expectations: "The most certain fact of all is that early Christianity was an eschatological movement."[3]

New Testament scholar Dale Allison agrees, arguing persuasively that Jesus placed himself as the central figure in the eschatological end-time drama. For Allison, the historical Jesus was not a poet speaking metaphorically about judgment; rather he lived and thought apocalyptically. Citing profusely from the gospels, Allison concludes that Jesus envisaged, as did many other Jews in his time and place, "the advent, after suffering and persecution, of a great judgment, and after that a supernatural utopia, the kingdom of God, inhabited by the dead come back to life, to enjoy a world forever rid of evil and wholly ruled by God. Further, he thought that the night was far gone, the day at hand."[4] The belief of early Christians in the imminence of the end, according to Allison, originated not from the church's post-Easter expectations, but with Jesus himself.

Marcus Borg represents a growing number of modern scholars who challenge this understanding of Jesus, envisioning instead a non-eschatological Jesus, whose role, if interpreted prophetically, should be limited to that of a social prophet engaged in radical social criticism. According to this model, Jesus was a counter-cultural revolutionary who opposed the domination systems of his day both in person and through an alternative community of disciples, chosen to represent the New Israel of God. In Borg's view the kingdom of God represents a this-worldly social vision—a vision that empowers Christians and defines the church's ongoing role in society—rather than an other-worldly eschatological vision imposed from above and occasioned by a church raptured from this earth, an interpretation popular in many American fundamentalist and evangelical circles today.

Since it is not pedagogically acceptable to commingle eschatological and noneschatological perspectives of Jesus, scholars feel forced to take sides. Either Jesus' mindset was eschatological or it was not, and for that reason modern scholarship does not allow fence-sitting on the matter. There is no question in my mind that Jesus was clearly driven by current Jewish

---

3. Sanders, "Jesus: His Religious Type," 6.
4. Allison, *The Historical Christ*, 95.

eschatological expectations and that he organized his ministry around those conceptions. As an eschatological prophet, however, he brought the entire package of prophecy to bear on his task, meaning that through his work and ministry he believed he was inaugurating and embodying the works of God's kingdom.

The Gospels and the Historical Jesus: Three Criteria

Biblical scholars famously distinguish between the "Jesus of history" and the "Christ of faith." While the New Testament writers had a great deal to say about the latter, what about the former? Who was Jesus of Nazareth? What did he teach, and what did he believe? The only way to know what Jesus actually taught is through the sources that survive from antiquity, namely, the four gospels. However, these books must be examined critically. To reconstruct the historical Jesus, it is not enough simply to quote verses from the Bible; every verse of the gospels must be examined carefully, not just to see what it says and to determine what it means, but more importantly, to establish whether it actually goes back to Jesus.

To establish reliability, biblical scholars have devised three major criteria for examining the gospels as historical sources for the life and teachings of Jesus. The first criterion used is called *independent attestation*. This criterion maintains that traditions that are attested independently by more than one source are more likely to be reliable than those found in only one source. The logic behind this criterion is that if two sources independently attest to a saying or deed of Jesus, then neither of them could have made it up. It is important to stress that the sources must be independent. The evidence they present is stronger than having only one witness. A saying found in both Matthew and Luke, however, is not independently attested, because both Matthew and Luke could have gotten it from Q (such as the Lord's Prayer or the beatitudes).[5] However, a saying found in both Mark and John, or in Luke and the noncanonical Gospel of Thomas, would be independently attested, because John did not use Mark, and Thomas did not use Luke. It is important to emphasize that independently attested

---

5. The Q source (from the German word *Quelle*, meaning "source") is a saying source said to underlie Matthew and Luke. While the existence of Q is hypothetical and disputed, since no copies have survived, scholars disagree on whether this source was originally written or merely oral.

traditions are not automatically authentic, only that they are more likely to be authentic.

Examples of this criterion include stories of Jesus associating with John the Baptist, which are found in Mark, Q, and John. Also included under this criterion are parables of Jesus in which he likens the kingdom of God to seeds sowed by a sower, attested in Mark, Q, and the Gospel of Thomas. Of course, this criterion cannot disprove a single reference or one that is not multiply attested, but can only be used to indicate which traditions are more likely to be historically accurate. Simply because the Lord's Prayer comes only from Q does not mean Jesus did not actually teach it to his disciples. Similarly, just because the parable of the Good Samaritan appears only in Luke does not mean that Jesus could not have said it.

The second criterion is called *dissimilarity*. This criterion suggests that traditions that appear to work against the vested interests of the Christians who were telling them are more likely to be historically accurate than those that Christians may have invented to suit their own purposes. The logic behind this criterion is that we know that Christians were altering, and sometimes even creating, stories about Jesus. They did so to make their own points about him. Thus, if a story does not advance the vested interests of the Christians telling it, then it is not a story they would have made up. Such stories, then, survive in the tradition precisely because they really happened.

Examples of this criterion include the tradition that Jesus came from Nazareth, since Nazareth was an insignificant place, or Galilee, which had no connection with the coming Messiah (see John 1:46; also 7:41). If Christians were to "make up" a place for Jesus to be born, it would probably be Bethlehem (the home of King David), or Jerusalem (the city of God). Other examples of this criterion include the tradition of Jesus as a carpenter (an occupation of low social status at the time), or that he was baptized by John (since this might suggest that he was a disciple and therefore spiritually inferior to John). Jesus' followers would not have created such accounts, or the story that he was betrayed by one of his own followers, or that he died by crucifixion, since no Jew expected the Messiah to be crucified as a criminal.

Like the criterion of independent attestation, this criterion can only be used to argue in favor of a tradition, not against it. It is problematic when it is used to argue that something didn't happen, such as when Jesus predicted that he would die in Jerusalem, since this is something he might have anticipated. However, Jesus' prediction that he would rise in three days does not meet this criterion, since that was exactly what his later followers said had happened. The best-case scenario, of course, is when a traditions passes both criteria. For a tradition to be credible, however, it also needs to pass a third criterion.

The final criterion is *contextual credibility*. It argues that no tradition about Jesus can be accepted as reliable if it cannot plausibly be situated in a first-century Jewish Palestinian context. The logic of this criterion is self-evident: what Jesus said and did must make sense in a particular historical and cultural context. Unlike the other criteria, this one is used to argue against certain traditions as historically implausible. For example, the Gospel of Thomas contains sayings that make perfect sense in the context of second-century gnosticism, but sound completely unlike what a first-century Jew in Palestine would have said. These things likely do not go back to Jesus. Another example is the discussion between Jesus and Nicodemus in John 3:3, in the saying about "being born from above," which Nicodemus understands to mean "being born again." That misunderstanding only makes sense in Greek, not in Aramaic, the language Jesus would have used. This criterion is particularly useful for understanding how Jesus understood himself and his role.

As we have seen, to understand Jesus, we must situate him in his own historical context. Jesus was a first-century Palestinian Jew, and as such lived in a period of foreign subjugation by Rome. One consequence of foreign subjugation of Palestine included the formation of Jewish sects such as the Sadducees and Pharisees, which exercised some power and offered religious options for Jews living at the time. The Essenes lived at the margins of society, maintaining their own purity through separation from institutional Judaism. Through unique lifestyle and fervent study of scripture, they lived in anticipation of the imminent apocalypse in which God would judge the world, thereby ending Roman rule and purifying Judaism. The Zealots emphasized Jewish autonomy and their divinely appointed duty to reestablish Israel as a sovereign state, by force if necessary.

Despite the somewhat favored treatment of Jews by Rome, Roman rule was nonetheless felt by many Palestinian Jews as an unbearable burden. Jews responded to Roman rule in a variety of ways, from silent protest to armed rebellion. During the first century CE, various Jewish prophets arose to speak against Rome as God's enemies and were often killed as troublemakers. One form of resistance ideology, apocalypticism, became prominent in the period. As we saw earlier, this ideology claimed that the forces of evil that were currently in charge of this world and responsible for its suffering would be overthrown by God in a mighty act of judgment. This imminent event was thought to be the prelude to the appearance of God's kingdom in a utopian age on earth. John the Baptist was an apocalyptic prophet of this sort, and we have compelling reasons for thinking that Jesus held such apocalyptic views.

Was Jesus an Apocalyptic Prophet?

The view that Jesus was an apocalypticist was first popularized by Albert Schweitzer in his 1906 classic text, *Quest of the Historical Jesus*. In this book Schweitzer showed how previous critical scholars had portrayed Jesus incorrectly, because they failed to recognize that he was an apocalypticist. When we examine our gospel sources critically, we find that Schweitzer was right. To understand Jesus correctly, it is important to follow a primary rule used by historians, namely, that we should prefer sources that are closest to the time of the events they narrate and that are not tendentious. In the case of Jesus, a clear perspective emerges when we examine the earliest sources at our disposal: Mark, Q, M (Mark's independent source), and L (Luke's independent source); all portray Jesus apocalyptically. Interestingly, later sources, such as John and the Gospel of Thomas, do not.

In the earliest accounts of Jesus' teachings we find numerous apocalyptic predictions: a kingdom of God will soon appear on earth, in which God will rule. The forces of evil will be overthrown, and only those who repent and follow Jesus' teachings will enter the kingdom. Judgment on all others will be brought by the Son of Man, a cosmic figure who may arrive from heaven at any moment. Jesus is said to have proclaimed this message in all of our earliest surviving sources.

This is clearly the case in Mark 1:15 and 13:14–27, the latter passage ending with Jesus' proclamation: "Truly I tell you, this generation will not pass away until all these things have taken place" (Mark 13:30). The same message is found in Luke 17:24, 26–27 and Matthew 24:27, 37–39 (this is Q material), Matthew 13:40–43 (M), and Luke 21:34–36 (L). Some of these apocalyptic traditions are toned down in later traditions. For instance, contrast Mark 9:1 with Luke 9:27 and then with Luke 17:21 (found only in Luke). In this later gospel, Jesus no longer says that his disciples will see the kingdom come in power, but only that the kingdom will arrive in the ministry of Jesus. In Luke 17:21, Luke has Jesus state that the kingdom is "in your midst." This clearly differs from Mark's earlier "coming with power" (Mark 9:1).

The author of Luke's gospel does not seem to think that the coming of a real kingdom would occur in the lifetime of Jesus' companions. Evidently, because he was writing after they had died, and he knew that the end had not come, he deals with the "delay of the end" by making changes in Jesus' predictions. Later sources eliminate the apocalyptic material altogether. Thus, in the gospel of John, the kingdom is not described as imminent but as already present to those who believe in Jesus (3:3, 36). Here, in passages written near the end of the first century, the older apocalyptic idea that a day of judgment is coming and that the dead will be resurrected at the end of the historical age is replaced by a newer view, that in Jesus a person can already experience eternal life (11:23–26). This "de-apocalypticizing" of Jesus' message continues into the second century, as we see in the Gospel of Thomas, which contains a clear attack on anyone who believes in a future kingdom on earth (sayings 3, 18, 118).

From this evidence a clear picture emerges. It appears that, when the expected end did not arrive, later Christians changed Jesus' message accordingly. However, when we examine the earliest sources, it is clear that Jesus was an apocalypticist. This certainly fits in with the specific criteria of contextual credibility, dissimilarity, and independent attestation. First-century Palestine had many apocalyptic Jews, some of whom left writings (such as the Essenes, who wrote the Dead Sea Scrolls). Other apocalyptic Jews were activists, including John the Baptist and prophets such as Theudas (see Acts 5:36–37) and "the Egyptian," mentioned by Josephus.

Some of the gospel references clearly pass the criterion of dissimilarity, such as Mark 8:38, in which Jesus talks about a cosmic judge of the earth (the Son of Man), without any suggestion that the reference is himself, even though early Christians did make this association, equating Jesus with the coming heavenly judge. That, however, is not what Jesus taught. In some cases he clearly did speak about himself using the term "son of man" (that is, son of a human), as a reference to his humanity, but when speaking about the future coming of the heavenly Son of Man, Jesus does not appear to have been speaking about himself.

Another passage that passes the criterion of dissimilarity is the parable of the Sheep and the Goats in Matthew 25, which indicates that at the apocalyptic judgment, the Son of Man will judge the nations based on how they live. Since this does not coincide with the view of Jesus' later followers, who believed that salvation comes only on the basis of faith in Jesus and his resurrection, not on the basis of good works, the passage was likely not created by Christians but goes back to Jesus.

The tradition about Jesus as an apocalypticist also passes the criterion of independent attestation, since Jesus is portrayed thus in Mark, Q, M, and L but not in later sources, such as John or the second century Gospel of Thomas. Each of those early sources are independent of one another and all portray Jesus apocalyptically.

In addition to meeting these criteria, one final piece of evidence seems convincing. Not only did Jesus begin his ministry apocalyptically, through association with the apocalyptic prophet John the Baptist, but his ministry concluded with apocalyptic Christian communities, such as those established by the apostle Paul, who believed he was living at the end of the age (see 1 Thess 4:13—5:10). If Jesus began his ministry as an apocalypticist, and if the first Christian communities were apocalyptic, then it seems most likely that the middle—Jesus' life and teaching—was also apocalyptic.

Jesus proclaimed that God's kingdom was coming to earth imminently (Mark 1:15). These words in Mark, the first words Jesus is recorded to have said in that gospel, provide a summary of Jesus' teaching. This would be a real kingdom with real rulers, a kingdom that would welcome some people but exclude others. Before the kingdom arrived, a scene of judgment would take place, in which the Son of Man, a cosmic figure from heaven, would appear to destroy God's enemies. This coming judgment would involve a massive reversal of fortunes; those who had prospered in this world through siding with evil would be displaced, but those who had suffered would be exalted. The judgment would come not only to individuals, but also to institutions and governments. In particular, the Jewish temple in Jerusalem, the heart of all institutional Jewish worship, would be destroyed.

Throughout his authentic teachings, when Jesus refers to the coming kingdom, he seems to mean an actual earthly kingdom, with actual rulers. Consider Jesus' teachings found in Q, perhaps our earliest source: "Truly I tell you, at the renewal of all things, when the Son of Man is seated on the throne of his glory, you who have followed me will also sit on twelve thrones, judging the twelve tribes of Israel" (Matt 19:28; cf. Luke 22:30). While the arrival of the kingdom was "good news" for Jesus' followers, it was not good news for everyone. In a mighty act of judgment, evil rulers would be toppled and punished, and the oppressed would be raised up (Luke 13:23–29; cf. Matt 8:11–12). This coming judgment would involve a serious reversal of fortune, one that makes sense in an apocalyptic context (Mark 10:31; Luke 13:30).

Likewise, Jesus' ethical teachings make best sense in an apocalyptic context. These teachings, however, have come down to us today as perfect examples of how people ought to live normally. Nevertheless, it is important for us to understand that the meaning of Jesus' ethical teachings might have been quite different in their original context from their meaning in ours. In our context, Jesus' teachings assist us in knowing how to get along with one another, so that we can contribute to a healthier and more wholesome society, allowing us to experience peace and wellbeing for the long haul. But for Jesus there was not going to be a long haul. The Son of Man would soon come in judgment, and people needed to prepare for entrance into his kingdom by showing that they sided with God rather than with the forces of evil that were opposed to him. Jesus' ethical teachings were ethics of the kingdom—they both reflected what life would be like in the kingdom and qualified one for entrance once it arrived.

In the kingdom, there would be no hatred; thus, people should love one another now. In the kingdom, there would be no oppression; thus, people should work for justice now. In the kingdom, there would be no war; thus, people should work for peace now. In the kingdom, there would be no sexism; thus, people should work for equality now. Only those who lived in ways that are appropriate to the kingdom would be allowed entrance when it arrived.

According to Jesus' teachings in the Sermon on the Mount, his followers should regard entrance into the kingdom as their most prized possession, and even be willing to give up all their possessions for the sake of the kingdom (Matt 6:25–33). Later on, Jesus indicates in his parable of the Precious Pearl (Matt 13:45–46) that the kingdom is like a merchant in search of fine pearls who finds a perfect pearl and then goes out and sells all that he has to buy it. The pearl is the kingdom, and it demands our ultimate allegiance; that's how valuable it is. For Jesus, nothing made sense apart from the kingdom of God that was on the verge of breaking into history. If its coming found one unprepared, all would be lost.

If Jesus' ethical teachings make best sense in an apocalyptic context, we need to rethink their meaning. Jesus, it appears, did not deliver timeless truths to guide individuals in leading long and productive lives. His teachings were meant to show people how to live in order to enter the kingdom that would soon appear. When we examine teachings such as "love your neighbor as yourself," and "love your enemies and pray for those who persecute you," he is teaching ethics of the coming kingdom. How else can we understand Jesus' teaching to the young ruler, that he should give up everything—all

Jesus and Jewish Eschatology

possessions and everything that binds one to this world (Mark 10:17–31)—except in this context? This emphasis on giving up everything for the kingdom means that Jesus was not a major proponent of what we now call "family values" (see Luke 14:26; 12:51–53). As with other hard sayings of Jesus,[6] these should not be explained away so that they no longer mean what they say. Instead, they should be placed in an apocalyptic context.

Understood apocalyptically, Jesus' command to love one's neighbor and God above all else points to the coming kingdom, when God will provide such things as food and clothing (Matt 6:25–33). To those who trust God, all things are possible, for that is how God will care for us in his kingdom that is soon to come. Jesus, then, did not see himself as inventing a new system of ethics, so much as explaining the Law of Moses in view of his own apocalyptic context.

While later sources have Jesus proclaiming the kingdom as a present reality, this is not what Jesus actually taught. For him, the kingdom was imminent, but it had not yet arrived. Understanding Jesus' message of the coming judgment of the Son of Man, including the destruction of the temple in Jerusalem, helps explain Jesus' actions in the temple prior to his crucifixion. Viewed apocalyptically, they become a symbolic expression of his teaching, a prophetic gesture or enacted parable of the coming of God's imminent judgment on the earth, beginning with institutional Judaism. In cleansing the temple, Jesus was demonstrating on a small scale what would soon occur in a large way.

Jesus was betrayed by one of his own followers, Judas Iscariot. What is not clear, though, is what it was that Judas betrayed, or why he acted as he did. Some believe that he betrayed Jesus for financial gain; others argue that Judas grew disillusioned when he realized that Jesus had no intention of becoming a political messiah; yet still others have reasoned that Judas wanted to force Jesus' hand, thinking that if Jesus were arrested, he would call out for support and start an uprising that would overthrow the Romans. While each of these explanations has merit, the clearest explanation is that Judas may have divulged insider information that the authorities could use to bring Jesus up on charges. Jesus, it appears, taught his disciples things in private that he did not state publicly.

We have several hints as to what Jesus taught about himself that Judas might have divulged to the authorities. Almost certainly, the charge leveled against Jesus by the Roman governor Pontius Pilate was that he considered

---

6. For an expanded discussion of Jesus' hard sayings, see chapter 12 below.

himself to be the King of the Jews (Mark 15:2; John 19:33; 19:19). However, Jesus never called himself this in any of the gospels. Why would he be executed for a claim he never made? Jesus did teach that after the Son of Man executed judgment on the earth, the kingdom would arrive. Kingdoms, by their nature, have kings. Who would be the king? Ultimately, of course, it would be God. However, Jesus probably did not think that God would physically sit on the throne in Jerusalem. Who, then, would?

The earliest traditions indicate that Jesus thought he would be enthroned. For one thing, only those who accepted his message would be accepted into the kingdom. Jesus also told his disciples that they would be seated on twelve thrones to rule the twelve tribes of Israel. Who would be over them? It was Jesus who had called them to be the Twelve. Moreover, his disciples asked him for permission to sit at his right hand and his left in the coming kingdom (Mark 10:37). Of course, the current textual context, as modified by later authors and redactors, changes the original meaning of Jesus' teaching. Rightly understood, his disciples would have viewed him as ruler in the kingdom, just as he was their "ruler" now.

Judas, then, betrayed this private teaching of Jesus to the Jewish authorities, and that explains why they could level the charges against Jesus that he called himself the Messiah, the King of the Jews. Of course, he meant it in the apocalyptic sense, but they meant it in a this-worldly sense. Once the local Jewish authorities learned this insider information, they had all the grounds they needed to make a quick arrest to get Jesus out of the public eye, and thus avoid any recriminations from their Roman overlords over disturbances caused by Jesus and his followers.

Questions for Discussion and Reflection

Having read chapter 8, answer the following questions, writing your answers in a journal. If you are in a group study, be prepared to share your answers with those in the group.

1. This chapter begins by discussing the pervasive influence of apocalyptic thinking upon Christians throughout history. In a sentence or two, define the word "apocalyptic." In your estimation, why have Christians been so attracted to this perspective?

2. Explain the hopes and fears embodied in apocalyptic eschatology, and how it emerged in postexilic Judaism.

Jesus and Jewish Eschatology

3. While apocalyptic eschatology can easily be labeled dualistic thinking, it need not be associated with metaphysical dualism. Explain the distinction between metaphysical and postcreation dualism.

4. In your estimation, what role did Jewish apocalyptic thinking play in shaping the early Christian movement?

5. Using biblical categories, explain why only God can initiate and bring about God's kingdom on earth.

6. In your estimation, are we living in the "last days"? Explain your answer.

7. Modern scholarship is divided regarding Jesus' self-understanding. Some scholars view Jesus to be an apocalyptic prophet, whereas others envision a non-apocalyptic Jesus. Scholars such as Marcus Borg suggests alternative models said to accurately portray Jesus' self-understanding: mystic, healer, wisdom teacher, and social critic. It has become all too easy to see Jesus in one's own image. Some see him as a wandering Cynic, others as a feminist, and still others as social or political liberator. How do you view Jesus, apocalyptically or non-apocalyptically? Explain your answer.

8. Given the many additions and changes that entered the Jesus story in the decades prior to and during the recording of the gospels, scholars have devised three historical criteria to reconstruct the life and teachings of the historical Jesus. Explain these criteria and assess their merit. Which, if any, do you find most convincing? Explain your answer.

9. What evidence strikes you as most convincing that Jesus was an apocalyptic prophet? How does this view differ from what you have previously understood about Jesus? Does understanding Jesus as an apocalypticist have any bearing on the relevance of Christianity in the modern world?

10. In your estimation, what is the connection between Jesus' ethical teachings and his apocalyptic perspective?

11. Which of Jesus' ethical teachings do you find most significant and transformative? Explain your answer.

9

The First Coming of Christ as Eschatological Event

THE NEW TESTAMENT IS saturated with the belief that something new has happened in the history of humanity, in and through the life and death of Jesus Christ, and above all through his resurrection from the dead. In order to make sense of the New Testament, we need to begin with Easter, for Easter is central to Christianity. Whatever occurred on that first Easter, it had incredible power. Before the Easter experience Jesus' followers forsook him and fled. After the Easter experience they were willing to die for their conviction that whatever their understanding of God, it had to include Jesus of Nazareth. This shift in God consciousness revolutionized the theology of a group of Jewish people so dramatically that the world has never been the same. In addition, the Easter event led Jewish Christians to create Sunday, a new holy day, different from yet fulfilling the notion of the Jewish sabbath.

The continued experience of God's presence in this community of faith was so real that in time even this experience was redefined. Through this definition the concept of the Holy Spirit and later the doctrine of the Trinity became the very cornerstone of the Christian faith. No matter how one understands the meaning of Jesus' resurrection and the message of Easter, there must be about it something real enough to account for these measurable effects.[1] But what really happened, and what does it mean?

When we examine the gospel accounts, which describe in some detail the event we call the resurrection, we find that they do not give a clear-cut

1. Spong, *Liberating the Gospels*, 278.

The First Coming of Christ as Eschatological Event

and harmonious picture as to what happened. The Easter narratives, taken literally, raise more questions than they answer. And so we dare to ask whether Paul and the authors who write about the resurrection, writers we call Mark, Matthew, Luke, and John, assumed the literal objective quality of the Easter stories as they described them. Is it possible, we must ask, to affirm the reality of the Easter experience without taking literally the details of the resurrection moment? This is a crucial and necessary distinction. Were the gospel stories of Easter written to capture a literal description of something that actually happened? Can Easter be real without this kind of objectivity?

When we look at the story of Jesus' life as the gospel writers portray it, particularly when they deal with the birth and death of Jesus, can we think that they intended their words to be understood literally? They were not writing history or biography. They were trying to interpret a life-changing experience that had been very real to them, but all they could use were limited human words. The gospel writers signaled this weakness of vocabulary to their readers by exaggerating their language to the point at which their words became literally absurd. The entire gospel narrative is illustrative of this, but it reaches a climax in the stories of Jesus' birth and death.

Symbolic language is obviously present in the story of Jesus' birth. Do virgins conceive? Do angels sing to shepherds? Do stars wander through the sky so slowly that magi can follow them? Would wise men travel with symbolic interpretive gifts for a newborn child, including myrrh as a sign of what that baby's eventual death would accomplish? Even in the first century these things would be recognized as the stuff of fairy tales, not unlike narratives of those who seek a pot of gold at the end of the rainbow.

The gospel narratives go on to relate accounts of Jesus walking on water, transforming five loaves of bread into enough food to feed multitudes, and even raise people from the dead. The narratives then culminate in tales describing the final events in Jesus' life. Were the graves of the "saints in Jerusalem" really opened by Jesus' death so that the bodies of those long deceased ones could rise up, be resuscitated, and walk the streets of that city in the sight of many (Matt 27:52)? Were these ever meant to be literal stories, even in the first century, or is there something else going on in these narratives that we miss because we have for so long been taught to read them as historical?

Did the risen Jesus miraculously appear out of thin air to the two people on the road from Jerusalem to Emmaus and then just as miraculously disappear into thin air after they had recognized him in the sacrament of

Living Water

the broken bread (Luke 24:13–35)? Did the risen Jesus walk through locked doors and barred windows to get into that upper room to join his disciples at the time of the evening meal on the first day of the week following the crucifixion (John 20:19–23)? If people really believed that Jesus could do that, why would the stone in front of the tomb have been a problem and thus why was angelic help needed to remove it?[2]

Once we get beyond the simple inadequacy of human language to describe the realm of the divine, we must then face the incongruities present in the biblical texts of Easter. How many angels were at the tomb? Was it one, as Mark and Matthew state, or were there two angels, as Luke and John assert? Where were the disciples when the reality of Easter first dawned on the disciples? Mark and Matthew indicate that they were in Galilee. Luke directly contradicted this understanding, insisting that every appearance of the risen Christ occurred in Jerusalem or in its environs. Did the women see the risen Lord at the tomb at the dawn of Easter? No, said Mark; yes, said Matthew; no, said Luke; yes, said John, but it was not "the women" but only one woman, and her name was Mary.[3]

Was the resurrected body of Jesus physical? Matthew seemed to think so when he portrayed the women taking hold of the feet of Jesus (Matt 28:9). Luke portrays Jesus as eating fish in the presence of the disciples and as inviting the disciples to handle him, claiming that a spirit does not have flesh and bones (Luke 24:39–43). Such descriptions sound quite physical. But in the Emmaus road account this body could appear out of thin air and disappear into thin air. John had the same internal conflict in his text. John's Jesus could walk into a locked room, but once inside he also offered his physical wounds for inspection (John 20:19–25). "Everywhere one turns in the biblical texts of Easter there is confusion, for assertions made in one gospel are contradicted in another."[4]

Next, we examine the order of resurrection appearances as given in 1 Corinthians 15:1–6. The first witness was Cephas (Peter), then the twelve, then five hundred witnesses, and last of all, Paul. In Mark, the first gospel to be written, there is no mention of an actual appearance of the risen Jesus. This gospel announces an anticipated reunion in an unspecified future (Mark 16:1–8). Matthew, writing more than twenty years after Paul, states that the first appearance was not to Cephas, but to the women in the

---

2. These questions are taken from the discussion in Spong, *Eternal Life*, 174–77.
3. Spong, *Liberating the Gospels*, 280–82.
4. Spong, *Liberating the Gospels*, 283.

The First Coming of Christ as Eschatological Event

garden. Later he describes an appearance to the eleven, not to the twelve, but he never relates an account of a moment when an appearance to Peter might have occurred (Matthew 28). Luke does affirm that Peter was the first (Luke 24:34); second in his listing, however, was not the appearance to the twelve, as Paul had asserted, but to an unknown man named Cleopas (Luke 24:13), who was traveling with a friend on the road to Emmaus. Only after this episode, according to Luke, did Jesus appear to the disciples (Luke 24:36). John, the last gospel to be written, mentions that the risen Christ appeared first to Mary Magdalene, and only second to the disciples, but not to all twelve, since both Thomas and Judas clearly were absent. No source in the biblical tradition corroborates Paul's mention of an appearance to five hundred brethren or to James.[5]

Ask yourself, if you are still confined to the literal sense of the story, why it is that though the Christian community attached great weight to the resurrection, no two accounts of it are alike? Also note why the described events are seen as taking place at the dawn of the day, and why the resurrection takes place privately and not publicly. Are we dealing, in these ancient biblical narratives, with a different level of reality and a different kind of language? How does one explore and seek to make rational sense out of experiences that occur at the edges of life? Do these questions not give us a clue that these writers were trying to say something that stretched ordinary human language beyond its normal limits? Surely these writers were aware that they were describing an internal, profoundly real and reorienting psychic and mystical experience that had altered human consciousness and, therefore, human history. Should we expend time and energy looking for proofs of the literalness of these details so that we can, first, convince ourselves that they are true, and then pass on that understanding to the next generation? Can our fear of death ever be transcended by these literalistic approaches? In each of the above-cited examples I would argue that the words were not, and were never intended to be, literal descriptions of real happenings, and that to treat them as if they were is to distort them.

Regardless of one's stance on these matters, one point is clear: Jesus appeared only to his followers; unbelievers did not see him. This should warn us against supposing that the resurrection was an objective event capable of being seen by all persons. Only in faith could one behold the risen Christ. To the church, the resurrection was the sign and assurance that God had won a decisive victory over "the law of sin and of death" (Rom 8:2) and

---

5. Spong, *Liberating the Gospels*, 280–81.

had made available "newness of life." Already believers could participate in the life of God's kingdom. As God raised Christ from the dead, so God had raised them from "death" in order that they might share, both now and hereafter, in the "new creation."

Up to this point we have attempted to project ourselves into the mindset of early Christians, who thought Hebraically about the resurrection. Since the Bible is written in an idiom more or less strange to us, we must learn the new language, lest we completely misunderstand the faith early Christians attempted to communicate. As noted in chapter 8, before the outbreak of the War of the Jews against Rome in 66 CE, Judaism held specific hopes for the future, including the restoration of the tribes of Israel; the conversion, destruction, or subjugation of the Gentiles; the renewal of Jerusalem, including a new or rebuilt temple; and the purification of God's people and their worship. Christians inherited the Hebraic view that history is the interval between the beginning and the end. This eschatology, however, was radically transformed by the Christian gospel, which affirmed that already the powers of God's kingdom had broken into history in the person of Jesus of Nazareth, above all in his death and resurrection. As Peter proclaimed on the day of Pentecost, quoting an eschatological passage from the prophecy of Joel, already men and women were living "in the last days" (Acts 2:16–21).

When we place the resurrection of Jesus into an apocalyptic context, it makes complete sense that it represents the new reality that is expected in the coming age. Jewish apocalypticists did not expect to be taken to heaven in the new age. Rather, that new age would be a golden age on earth. Associated with this expectation was the belief that when the time had been fulfilled for the current evil age, there would be a general resurrection of the dead (see Matt 27:51–53). Followers of Jesus who believed in the resurrection of Jesus would draw an obvious conclusion, namely, that the new age had already begun. In 1 Corinthians, Paul makes this connection, finding in the resurrection of Jesus clear proof of the anticipated general resurrection of the dead (1 Cor 15:12–24). In Paul's mind, Jesus was the "first fruits" of resurrection, that is, the beginning of God's final winnowing or harvesting process. This meant, for Paul and other early Christian apocalypticists, that God's end-time judging and rewarding was to occur shortly. Jesus had been exalted to heaven, but would soon return as the heavenly Son of Man to judge the earth.

The First Coming of Christ as Eschatological Event

During his lifetime, Jesus had spoken of the coming Son of Man as a divine emissary, not to be equated with himself. Now, however, his followers began thinking of him, not as a prophetic forerunner of the final apocalypse, but as the actual coming judge referred to in Daniel 7:13-14. Whereas Jesus had taught his disciples that he would have a place of prominence in the coming kingdom, after the Resurrection his followers assumed that the kingdom had already begun, and that Jesus was already its ruler. In fact, Jesus was now ruler of all things in heaven and earth. No longer merely King of the Jews, they now understood him to be Lord of all.

Like their Old Testament counterparts, the followers of Jesus were shaped by an event so profound that it continues to be celebrated as decisive for Christians around the world. The early Christians found in Easter a correlation with the exodus—a path from darkness to light, despair to hope, inability to possibility, bondage to freedom—and with creation, for the resurrection constituted a new beginning for humanity.

While the line between the eschatology of Jesus and that of the church cannot be clearly drawn, it seems likely that Jesus thought in the framework of Jewish apocalyptic, though purging it of features such as nationalism, revenge on enemies, and desire for a sensuous paradise. While he seemed to have conceived his messianic role to be that of Isaiah's Suffering Servant, quite likely he also related himself to the figure of the coming Son of Man, Daniel's heavenly figure who would appear on the clouds at the consummation of history (Mark 14:62; see Dan 7:13-14). In any case, early Christians clearly believed that the appearance of the Messiah in the role of the Suffering Servant was an eschatological event. It was their conviction that already the *eschaton* had entered history, giving assurance of the near approach of the Day of Judgment and "the time of universal restoration" (Acts 3:20-21). The cross was God's sentence of judgment upon human sin and all the powers of darkness, but God's victory in the resurrection had already made possible a "new creation" for those who were in Christ (2 Cor 5:17).

Christian Transformation of Apocalyptic

While early Christians shared basic convictions with Jewish apocalyptic, one finds not only similarities but also striking differences. For example, the New Testament transformed the Jewish apocalyptic perspective by announcing that God has done something totally and radically new through the life, death, and resurrection of Jesus Christ. A "new creation" has begun to appear.

The New Testament portrays Jesus not merely as an apocalyptic visionary who announces the mystery of God's kingdom to a select few; rather, he himself is the sign of God's kingdom in the present historical age. Jesus' crucifixion, crowned with resurrection, signifies that Jesus is the victor in the long struggle with evil. The New Testament announces that the period of waiting is over, for the king has come and the dominion of God has already been inaugurated. In other words, the Christian gospel has altered the time scheme of apocalyptic, with its sharp separation of "the present evil age" from "the age to come," so that the old must pass away before the new can come. In the New Testament, the two ages are like overlapping circles, for already God has introduced the new age through Jesus Christ even while the old age persists. In the Christian reinterpretation of apocalyptic, the supreme sign of the new age is the resurrection of Christ from the dead. As Paul argues in 1 Corinthians 15, this end-time event has already occurred in the midst of the present age. So near and certain is God's triumph that Paul can go so far as to say that not everyone will die (1 Cor 15:51; likewise, Matthew's gospel refers to a strange apocalyptic event occurring at the moment when Jesus was crucified, when many who were dead are said to have come forth from their graves; 27:51–54).

To be sure, the Christian community lives in the tension of the "already" and the "not yet." Using the symbolic language of apocalyptic, the trumpet signaling God's final triumph has not yet sounded. There is still a period of waiting for the final consummation, the coming of God's kingdom fully on earth and the appearance of Jesus Christ in glory. But this waiting is not the expectation of counting the days or speculating on an apocalyptic timetable. For already God's triumph has been manifest in the resurrection of Christ.

Finally, "apocalyptic has given to the early Christian community a profound grasp of the meaning of God's triumph in Jesus Christ. God's victory is liberation from the power of sin through divine forgiveness, displayed in the vicarious and atoning death of Jesus. The apocalyptic perspective, however, pushes Christian interpreters to go beyond the prophetic message of sin and forgiveness and to proclaim God's triumph over all the powers of darkness, chaos, evil, and death."[6] Paul lists some of those powers in his

---

6. Anderson, *Contours of Old Testament Theology*, 335.

The First Coming of Christ as Eschatological Event

great victory proclamation at the end of Romans 8, where he declares that through Christ we are "more than conquerors" (Rom 8:37).

The call to conquer is fundamental to the structure and theme of the book of Revelation, the apocalypse that brings the Christian canon to a close. Everything that is said in the seven messages to the churches has this aim, expressed in the promise to the conquerors that concludes each (Rev 2:7; 11, 17, 28; 3:5, 12, 21). Like Jesus, the real victors are the martyr-witnesses, those who are faithful to God even to the point of death. Conquering is not represented as something to which only some are called, but as the only way for Christians to reach their eschatological destiny. According to Revelation 21:7–8, there are only two options: to conquer and inherit the promises, or to suffer the second death in the lake of fire. John's message in Revelation is a call for resistance against evil, not, however, through violence but through kingdom living and witnessing.

While later Christians focused on the vision of a Second Coming of Christ, it is important to recognize that in the early Christian message the center of gravity lay not in the anticipation of Christ's return but in the proclamation that Christ's "first coming" was itself an eschatological event. The New Testament places the emphasis on the victory that has already been won in the cross and resurrection and shuns any attempt to pry into the mystery of the future which lies in the sole authority of God (Acts 1:7; Matt 24:26). Oscar Cullmann expressed this matter aptly using an analogy from World War Two. Speaking of the invasion at Normandy, known as the Decisive Day (D-day), he noted that the decisive battle in a war may occur at a relatively early stage of the war, and yet the war continues. While the war continues until Victory Day (V-day), the tide turns on D-day, guaranteeing the final outcome.[7] As a result of Christ's resurrection, early Christians were assured that the goal of history had been achieved proleptically by Christ's victory over death. The End would merely vindicate the faith of the present.

At the cross, one of the seven last sayings of Jesus is "It is finished" (John 19:30), a statement not of resignation but of accomplishment. At a certain point the earthly career of Jesus of Nazareth came to an end; what he accomplished would not be done again or anew. Nevertheless, with God every end is a new beginning. The end of Jesus known in the flesh is the beginning of Christ known in the Spirit. It is faith in this living Christ, encountered through the living Spirit, that keeps New Testament hope alive.

---

7. Cullmann, *Christ and Time*, 84.

The Kingdom of Heaven

For those interested in understanding how Jesus' teachings on the kingdom affect faith and practice, a good place to begin is the Sermon on the Mount, found in Matthew 5–7 (an abbreviated and revised version appears in Luke's Sermon on the Plain; 6:17–49). This so-called "sermon" should not be considered as having been delivered by Jesus on one occasion, but was most likely formed by the author of Matthew's gospel for his community, gathered from collections of memorized sayings of Jesus. Some find here a new moral code, to be followed literally, while others, noting the severity of the standards, call them "interim ethics," supposing that Jesus' envisioned them as rules applicable only in a time of crisis.[8]

At the heart of the Sermon on the Mount we find these words: "But strive first for the kingdom of God and his righteousness" (Matt 6:33). According to this teaching, the kingdom is to be the believer's first and main concern. It was certainly so for Jesus, who gave up everything for the sake of the kingdom.

Finding myself among the many biblical scholars fascinated by Jesus' teaching on the kingdom, I too have been attracted to this concept, in part because of its enigmatic nature. While doing research on this topic, I came across Morton Kelsey's book *Afterlife*, and found in it a unique understanding of the kingdom, one I had never heard before. According to Kelsey, "the central message of Jesus of Nazareth is about heaven."[9] With that statement, Kelsey indicates that when Jesus used the phrase "kingdom of God," he was speaking about heaven directly rather than indirectly about God's presence or God's rule.[10]

My initial reaction upon reading Kelsey's statement was perplexity, for it sounded like something I had heard repeatedly through the course of my life and had rejected, namely, that the main concern of Christians on earth should be about how to get to heaven. But that is not what Kelsey meant.

---

8. Albert Schweitzer coined the phrase "interim ethics" to express his belief that Jesus understood himself to be living at the end of human history. The interim period was to be short; hence the stern ethic.

9. Kelsey, *Afterlife*, 157.

10. As is commonly known, the gospel of Matthew often substitutes the expression "kingdom of heaven" for "kingdom of God," using "heaven" as a circumlocution for "God." The usual explanation for this peculiarity is that Matthew was writing primarily to a Jewish audience, which preferred to address God or to speak about God indirectly rather than directly, using terms such as "The Name" or "heaven" as substitutes for "God" or for "deity."

The First Coming of Christ as Eschatological Event

As he states, when Jesus spoke about heaven, those who heard him were amazed, because Jesus' message differed "in two ways from anything they had heard before. They knew about hoping for heaven in the future and trying their best to earn it and avoid punishment. But Jesus spoke about finding heaven within and around and among us, as well as in a future hidden from us. Heaven, he said, is at hand. . . . Heaven, Jesus taught, can be shared in the here and now. It is both the immediate goal toward which we work in this life, and also the gift we hope to be given in the end."[11] What Mark and Luke call "the kingdom of God," what Matthew calls the "kingdom of heaven," and what John calls "eternal life," is a reality both present now and hereafter, both immanent and transcendent.

According to Kelsey, the key to understanding the nature of the kingdom, that is, the key to understanding what heaven is like, is given at the start of the Sermon on the Mount. Because Jesus spoke of the kingdom (heaven) repeatedly, using a variety of images to speak of the concept, the best place to go for a comprehensive view, for a blueprint or working plan of the kingdom, is the eight beatitudes found in Matthew 5:3–12.

Whether this passage is directly from the mouth of Jesus or a summary by those well acquainted with his teaching makes little difference. Either way, it summarizes Jesus' teaching about the kingdom, highlighting the qualities that characterize those who experience God in the present and in the afterlife. The blessed, or fortunate, are those who encounter God in life and therefore find ultimate meaning.

A reading of the beatitudes indicates that the result or reward is the same in the first and in the last beatitude ("for theirs is the kingdom of heaven," Matt 5:3, 10). These identical promises enclose the six intervening statements like parentheses. It seems reasonable, then, to take all eight statements as descriptions of God's kingdom, the kingdom of heaven. What Jesus tells us in this passage, then, is two things: the nature of heaven, and the fact that we can participate initially in its reality now and more fully after death.

Keys to the Kingdom of Heaven[12]

The eight qualities found in the beatitudes—the poor in spirit, those who mourn, the meek, those who hunger and thirst for righteousness, the

---

11. Kelsey, *Afterlife*, 157–58.
12. This segment is adapted from Kelsey, *Afterlife*, 186–211.

merciful, the pure in heart, the peacemakers, and those who are persecuted for righteousness' sake—are not steps that individuals must take consecutively to reach the fortunate or blessed state, but are more like keys to doors, "any one of which will swing open and let a person enter the kingdom of heaven."[13]

Entrance into the kingdom is not what we ordinarily think. The world of Jesus Christ, of heavenly spirituality, is unlike ordinary human standards. As Jesus saw it, we do not enter the kingdom because we are wise or powerful or intelligent, but rather because we are childlike and seeking, aware that all is not well. In the kingdom, the first are last and the last first. If it is the dispossessed and unfortunate, the gentle and merciful, who become citizens of the kingdom, how then can ordinary individuals prepare for the world we call heaven, where God dwells? The descriptions that Jesus gave in the beatitudes point the way. Here we find the kind of attitudes and actions that will enable us to experience the kingdom here and now. And these are the attitudes and actions that will allow us to share fully in that same kingdom after death.

Each of us has his or her redeeming quality. According to Carl Jung's depiction of personality types, the sensing person has the virtue of simplicity, the intuitive person of wisdom, the thinking type of justice, and the feeling person of joy. In addition, each person has a unique way of entering the kingdom, and each must find the doorway that represents entrance. Let us examine the eight keys to the kingdom that Jesus describes in the beatitudes and see what pattern of life they suggest.

- *The poor in spirit*. This quality, while it includes those who are materially poor, refers primarily to those who are inwardly poor, that is, those whose spirits are not inflated and arrogant. Because they are often detached from worldly attachments, the poor in spirit are open to new dimensions of reality. They are aware of inner conflict and realize that they cannot cope without saving help. The teachings of Jesus repeatedly stress that the surest way to gain one's life or one's self-esteem is to lose it, while those who continue to put their own pride and self-conceit first will end up losers. What this means for us today is that our most valiant efforts to hold the right beliefs and to do the right thing will fail if they result in self-satisfaction and arrogance. The moment we think we can earn God's favor, the door to spiritual

---

13. Kelsey, *Afterlife*, 187.

The First Coming of Christ as Eschatological Event

development begins to close. Only those who can accept the kingdom as a gift, unearned and unmerited, are able to enter.

- *Those who mourn.* Many events make us feel the emotion of sorrow; the most common is bereavement, the loss of someone we love. However, one may also grieve loss of security, honor, or position. Others mourn because there is so much suffering in the world, and they feel helpless to make a difference. Jesus often speaks of repentance; he asked people first to confront themselves, and then to react with regret and sorrow. The sorrowful are those who mourn over their inner and outer poverty and allow repentance to permeate their whole being. As it does, something happens to them, and a new kind of life begins to emerge. Grief is cured only as we pass through it, not through avoidance. Bearing sorrow and grief enlarges one's heart. Only those who pass through sorrow and mourning can help others face similar problems.

- *The meek.* The gentle or the meek include the poor in spirit and those who mourn. Such people are not puffed up with pride or arrogance but are humble, considerate, and unassuming. They treat others as equals, and they work to create conditions that allow others to develop more fully their capacities. The meek are resourceful and hopeful, facilitators who do not force their own goals onto others but rather accept others as they are. Gentleness, however, is not weakness. This quality of life is more like the resilience of a reed growing by a stream. The reed bends with the wind and survives. Even a gale cannot uproot it, while the mighty oak may be torn from its roots and left to die.

- *Those who hunger and thirst for righteousness.* "Hunger" and "thirst" speak of the human desire to seek fulfillment of the deep searching of the human heart. To hunger and thirst means to desire something strongly. In kingdom language, these terms refer to one's love for God. In John's account of the feeding of the five thousand, Jesus spoke of bread from heaven and told the people, "I am the bread of life. Whoever comes to me will never be hungry, and whoever believes in me will never be thirsty" (John 6:35). In the New Testament, righteousness is more than simply moral and legal aspects of right thinking and action. Paul suggests that people do not become righteous simply by following the law, but rather by accepting God's grace humbly. According to scripture, one becomes righteous when one hungers and thirsts for fellowship with God.

- *The merciful.* Most of us find it difficult to be merciful, for mercy involves forgiveness, and it is not easy to forgive those who hurt us. Jesus was clear about the importance of mercy and forgiveness. In the Lord's Prayer he included only one condition: we can expect God to give freely all that we need, including forgiveness, so long as we are able to forgive others. Charles Williams wrote in his book *The Forgiveness of Sins* that there are things that need not be forgiven, things that ought to be forgiven, and things that cannot be forgiven—and that the Christian is to forgive them all. How do we achieve this quality of life? Mercy flows naturally from a life marked by meekness and poverty of spirit.

- *Pure in heart.* We have a tendency to think of the heart in medical terms, as an organ that pumps blood through the body. The Greek language, however, views the heart as the center and source of inner life. It gives rise to all that makes us human. To be "pure" is to be sincere and single-minded. In his book *Purity of Heart*, the Danish philosopher Søren Kierkegaard suggested that purity of heart means to be directed toward one goal, to be motivated by one central passion. Within each of us are many different powers and voices, different desires competing for control. Our task, as followers of Christ, is to bring this motley crew together into one, undivided personality. This cannot happen unless we realize our poverty of spirit and pray to have all parts of our being brought together into harmony by an act of God's grace. In his teaching, Jesus warned that no one can serve two masters (Matt 6:22–24), and that every kingdom divided against itself cannot stand (Matt 12:25). Purity of heart, like poverty of spirit and righteousness, is a gift given to those who realize they are unable to satisfy the hunger and thirst of their souls. Purity of heart, however, is more than an attitude, a condition, or a state of life. It is the willingness to know oneself and to bring every aspect of one's life into harmonious relation with the kingdom and its goals.

- *The peacemakers.* In the Lord's Prayer we ask for God's will to be done and for God's kingdom to come on earth as it is in heaven. Peacemakers are committed to this goal. They work not only to bring harmony and peace to those around them but also to experience harmony and health within. Those who taste God's love come to know the peace— the harmony and blessed joy—that is an essential quality of God's kingdom. Such people are called children of God. As peacemakers,

The First Coming of Christ as Eschatological Event

they share in the nature of God. Growing in peace within, they also work to bring peace to others.

- *Those who are persecuted for righteousness' sake.* Jesus warned his followers that discipleship might lead to opposition and persecution. While society has changed since the first century, particularly in the West, where Christianity is the norm, the world still has ways of showing contempt for those who desire more than conventional religion. While such suffering can open a door into God's kingdom, this does not mean that we can find that doorway by inviting persecution or martyrdom. The church condemns all forms of violence and self-destructiveness, even that of martyrdom. The way of the kingdom, the way of the cross, requires courage as well as meekness. Meekness without courage can become weakness and sentimentality. Those who cannot enter the kingdom by way of peacemaking, humility, or mourning can enter through the door of courage, steadfastness, and forbearance.

The Blessings of the Kingdom of Heaven[14]

As with the eight qualities of the kingdom, the six results[15] describe blessings both present and future, the results found among those who are able to live in contact with God as the source of ultimate meaning. In the beatitudes Jesus is giving us his picture of God's kingdom, for whose coming we are to pray daily (Matt 6:10). What, then, are the blessings available to those who make God's kingdom, that is, relationship with God, a priority? These six qualities represent the best picture of heaven, of God's kingdom, ever given:

- *They will be comforted*, that is, they will be healed of all sorrow and anguish. The Greek word "to comfort or console" is the word from which "paraclete" or "comforter" is taken, a reference in John's gospel to the Holy Spirit. The person who is comforted is not just soothed and relieved of misery, but is strengthened, reconstituted, and re-established. Those who are comforted begin to see life more from God's

---

14. This segment is adapted from Kelsey, *Afterlife*, 168–85.

15. As noted above, two of the eight results or rewards are identical ("for theirs is the kingdom of heaven"), leaving six distinct results.

perspective, from an eternal stance; it is the state of reality in which the victory of Jesus' resurrection is reaffirmed and realized.

- *They will inherit the earth*, that is, they will be committed to improving the state of things here on earth. As heirs, they will work with God to provide the care God's earth needs.

- *They will be filled*, that is, they will experience wholeness and wellbeing. The word in Greek for "being filled" comes from the word for hay and was used to describe cattle being filled and satisfied. If you have ever seen a cow eat, you will note that a cow gets filled slowly and gradually. To be filled, we must acquire patience: too much too fast may well choke us. As Augustine put it, God made us for himself, and we cannot know rest or satisfaction until we find it in God. The best pictures of the kingdom—of heaven—suggest that we shall be slowly transformed through eternity, until we become the kind of people we have always wanted to be. Then we shall find visions of new potentials and gradually move toward new goals, each filling more complete than the last.

- *They will receive mercy*, that is, they will experience unconditional forgiveness. God is not just, but merciful. Heaven—the kingdom—is not a place of retribution, but a place of forgiveness, mercy, and love. Only as we experience love and forgiveness in our ordinary lives do we begin to understand that this is what God and God's eternal kingdom are like. Hell, as someone has said, can be described as a state of eternal obsession with guilt, so that one is unable to accept forgiveness. The unique idea of Christianity is that humans do not need to suffer from guilt and self-condemnation. Heaven is the state of being in which we are given a fresh start.

- *They will see God*, that is, they will experience the Beloved. Here on earth we must be content with experiencing the presence of God; in eternity we shall come "face to face with the Love that lights our inner being."[16] When we come to the center, finding there the source of all things, we will know that we are accepted, loved, desired.

- *They will be called children of God*, that is, they will accept their service in life like the pure play of children, full of joy, fun, and excitement. The children of God are also God's co-workers, and this is what

---

16. Kelsey, *Afterlife*, 179.

makes them inheritors of earth. Each image speaks of a different aspect of the same truth. Children, sons and daughters, not only rest with their parents, they also work and play with them. In a similar way, in heaven we can expect joy and fulfillment as well as participation in all of God's activity.

Paul, in speaking about heaven, can only grasp at straws when he says, "No eye has seen, nor ear heard, nor the human heart conceived, what God has prepared for those who love him" (1 Cor 2:9). Neither an eternal life that is already fully achieved here below, nor an eternal life begun and known solely in the beyond, satisfies our deepest spiritual longing. Only an eternal life already begun and truly known in part here, though fully achieved and completely understood hereafter, corresponds to the deepest longing of our human spirit as touched by God. May that, dear reader, be your experience, now and forever.

If we understand the kingdom correctly, God, it seems, appears far more interested in communicating with us than we are in communicating with God. God has taken the initiative by creating a spiritually rich universe, one that provides multiple pathways for contact, relationship, and even intimacy. The ball is in our court. How will we respond?

Questions for Discussion and Reflection

Having read chapter 9, answer the following questions, writing your answers in a journal. If you are in a group study, be prepared to share your answers with those in the group.

1. From an eschatological perspective, explain the shift in consciousness that occurred in the hearts and minds of Jesus' disciples as a result of the Easter event.

2. After reading this chapter, do you believe the gospel stories of Easter capture a literal description of what actually happened? Explain your answer.

3. After reading this chapter, do you believe the gospel stories of Jesus' birth capture a literal description of what actually happened? Explain your answer.

4. After reading this chapter, do you believe the gospel stories of Jesus' miracles capture a literal description of what actually happened? Explain your answer.

5. If a literal account of the resurrection of Jesus was important to early Christians, why is it that no two accounts are alike?

6. In practical terms, explain the meaning of the resurrection of Jesus (the Easter victory) in your life. How does this doctrine or event influence, benefit, or expand your self-understanding, how you cope with life, and your hope for the future?

7. In your estimation, how was the kingdom of God evident in the life, death, and resurrection of Jesus?

8. Explain Oscar Cullmann's analogy of D-day and V-day to explain the connection between the resurrection of Jesus and the goal of history.

9. What is your current understanding of "heaven"? Do you find it better to speak of heaven as a present reality on earth, as both a present (earthly) and future (eternal) reality, or as only a future reality? Explain your answer.

10. Read some of the more familiar teachings of Jesus, such as the beatitudes in Matthew 5:3–12, the Lord's Prayer in Matthew 6:9–13, and the parable of the Sheep and the Goats in Matthew 25:31–46, and reflect on what they would mean in an apocalyptic context.

11. With which of the beatitudes do you most relate? Which one seems most attractive? Explain your answer.

10

Jesus' Use of Parables

To STIMULATE INTEREST IN the kingdom and to help his audience anticipate its coming, Jesus taught in parables.[1] In this regard, a good starting point for understanding Jesus' use of parables is Mark 4:10–12 (see also Matt 13:13; Luke 8:10; and John 12:37). Thanks to John Bowker's landmark 1974 article on Mark 4:1–20, there is now widespread consensus in biblical scholarship that the parable of the Sower (Mark 4:3–8) and its interpretation (4:14–20) should be understood as an exposition of Isaiah 6.[2] According to Mark 4:10–12, it is not God who seeks to thwart understanding or turning to the truth but the hardness of heart and unwillingness to hear latent in many individuals. In his teaching here Jesus draws a parallel

---

1. Throughout the various stages of historical Jesus studies, scholars have agreed that parables represent an authentic voice of Jesus, viewing them as the "bedrock" and "core" of Jesus' teaching. This general consensus in scholarship has been questioned recently by John P. Meier. In volume 5 of his *A Marginal Jesus* series, he argues unconvincingly that the historical Jesus rarely told parables, and that only four demonstrably authentic parables appear in the gospels. While it is clear that the gospels are not neutral documents, they are witnesses to the life, ministry, and teaching of Jesus, and like all faith language, they are based on a combination of belief, fact, experience, and memory. While the historical Jesus cannot be recovered by scholarship, we cannot go to the opposite extreme and claim that the gospels are hypothetical, inauthentic, or unreliable by nature. Clearly the parables have been shaped, applied, adapted, restructured, and grouped by Christian authors, editors, and by faith communities, and few trained scholars would argue that they contain the *ipsissima verba* (the literal words) of Jesus. While scholars can identify redactional traits and theological and literary tendencies, they cannot demonstrate origin or creation.

2. Bowker, "Mystery and Parable," 311.

with the recalcitrance of Israel in Isaiah's time to heed prophetic warning. Mark's redaction shows that he also seeks to stimulate hearing.

Let us be clear: we cannot take the words in Mark 4:11-12 at face value, for the very reason that no words could more flatly deny the "mind of Christ." Jesus came to illumine hearts, minds, and lives and not to darken them; and because lives are self-darkened, he spoke in parables, well knowing that the rays of a parable can penetrate where ordinary words or doctrines can fail. In this respect, Matthew's version of Isaiah 6:9-10 in 13:10-15 is a vast improvement. Jesus spoke in parables not in order that people might be blinded but because they are blind, and in order that they might see, as Mark 4:33 makes clear: "With many such parables he spoke the word to them, as they were able to hear it."

While many interpreters conclude that "those outside" in Mark 4:11 are the crowds, while the disciples are the ones inside, this does not fit well with Mark's gospel overall. The crowds around Jesus hear him gladly, and the opposition comes from the religious leadership and his own family (3:21-25; 7:6-7). Significantly, the same language of hardness of heart and of having eyes and not seeing and ears and not hearing is used of the twelve disciples in 8:17-18 (see also 6:52). It is the stance of willingness to hear and obey that determines whether one is outside or inside. As we have seen in Mark 4:33, the purpose of parables is to demonstrate, enlighten, and enable hearing. In Mark 3:23 we are told that Jesus used parables as summons, inviting his opponents to change their thinking.

John Bowker suggests we interpret the phrase "in parables" at the end of Mark 4:11 not to exclude but to make clear the nature and character of those who hear. Parables do that; they confront, engage, force thought, and promote action, but they do so metaphorically, often in a veiled way, and especially in a context of opposition, saying indirectly what cannot be said openly. They can be mysterious, but if so, it is to stimulate thought. Thus, they both hide and reveal. Jesus taught in parables as did effective prophets, to appeal and to enable hearing. Where parables find a willing response, further explanation is given; where there is no response, the message falls on deaf ears and is lost.

Parables are not always obvious and self-explanatory, but even when enigmatic, their purpose is to enlighten. There is no logic or code to unlock to prove spiritual truth; there is only the prophetic opening of a window in the hope that shuttered eyes might look upon the kingdom, rule, and love of God. The parables as spoken by Jesus are such a window.

Jesus' Use of Parables

As Jesus seems to indicate—at least in Mark 4:11—parables are intended for people in first half of life religion, concerned with rules, regulations, restrictions, and boundaries. According to Mark's gospel, mature disciples don't need story theology, for they are already gifted with wisdom and insightful understanding ("to you has been given the secret [mystery] of the kingdom of God"). To clarify, the word "mystery" (or what the NRSV translates as "secret") did not in Jesus' Semitic world refer to what is mysterious and unknown, but rather to revelation, to what would be unknown if God did not reveal it. The mystery in Mark 4:11 has to do with people's reception of the message. Jesus' parables reveal the nature of God's kingdom (God's will) and provide handles for grasping it.

Speaking about the radical nature of the kingdom and the ever-present newness in the gospel, in Luke 5:38–39 Jesus notes that no one puts new wine in old wineskins, but rather that "new wine must be put into fresh wineskins." While with wine, aged wine is better than unaged wine—the old better than the new—in spiritual matters, God's newness is preferable to the old traditions. In the natural world, wineskins exist only for the wine. In spiritual matters, the new wine represents God's truth, which is ever new and fresh, and the old wine represents the traditions and the culture that we have inherited. As Jesus indicates, in spiritual matters traditions become hardened or frozen into prejudicial ways of thinking and living. Because we are God's vessel (wineskin), if God's new wine comes forth and we are unwilling to change, we will "burst," meaning we will be unable to contain God's fresh, transforming wine. Likewise, unless we are willing to change—to become new—we too will self-destruct.

Jesus understood the principle that was working against him in his own life. He was coming with the good news of the gospel that was totally new not only to his generation but to many in our time as well. As a result, we reject both the message and the messenger. The new teaching Jesus brings cannot be forced into old systems. To attempt to force his teaching into the traditions of Judaism, Catholicism, Protestantism, or any other of the world's religions or institutions simply does not work (see Matt 24:4–5; Rom 6:5–6; 16:17–18; Gal 1:6–10; Eph 4:14; 5:6–11; 1 Tim 6:3–5; Heb 13:9). In such cases, what is new will simply be manipulated, coerced, changed, or disregarded by the pre-existent tradition. Rather than becoming living water, such a gospel will merely become stagnant and stop flowing.

When we think of Jesus' parables, we ordinarily think of the Prodigal Son or the Good Samaritan, classic stories about how God relates to humans and how they should relate to one another. However, many, if not most of the parables, are distinctly eschatological in nature. These parables have a prophetic element, in that they tend to reverse conventional values rather than reinforce them. Though many parables reflect "wisdom from below," the source is "from above," for the means of the expressed counter-order is the inbreaking eschatological kingdom of God.

The parable of the Yeast in Matthew 13:33 (also Luke 13:20–21) is misleading as translated in the NRSV: "The kingdom of heaven is like yeast that a woman took and *mixed in with* three measures of flour until all of it was leavened," since the original Greek speaks of yeast that is "hidden in" the measures of flour. Could this story be about Jesus' mission, about how he is planting (hiding) the kingdom message in his audience through his *meshalim*? The woman kneading the dough may also be seen as an allusion to wisdom. In either case, the parable reflects an eschatological optimism about how things will finally turn out.

The parable of the Good Samaritan (Luke 10:29–37), one of Jesus' most beloved parables, has been called an "example story" (as a story teaching about human relations; that is, as a model to imitate or avoid; see 10:37, "Go and do likewise") rather than a comparative *mashal*, since it appears only in Luke, and only Luke contains example stories (10:30–37; 12:16–21; 16:19–31; 18:10–14). Furthermore, the parable exhibits clear marks of editorial activity (10:29, 36–37). Despite Luke's editorializing, this story likely goes back to Jesus, who intended it not as an example of "proper" behavior but as a counter-order *mashal*, a parabolic portrayal of how the inbreaking of the kingdom of God transforms people and reorders their thinking. The focal point of the story cannot be the Samaritan's good deed of kindness or compassion, since the Samaritan exceeds all bounds, "not merely ethnic bounds, but even the suggested bounds in the Old Testament of what compassion would look like."[3] What we have here is an ethnic reversal, used to challenge current attitudes regarding ritual standards. The notion of a "good Samaritan" was a contradiction in terms for a traditional Jew, but such reversal is typical of Jesus the sage, "who seems to specialize in oxymorons like good leaven, light burdens, and here a good Samaritan."[4]

The underlying issue in this parable is ritual holiness. There is surely some degree of contrast here between the Samaritan and the priest and Levite, the latter paragons of holiness and virtue in Jewish society. Both

---

3. Witherington, *Jesus the Sage*, 195.
4. Witherington, *Jesus the Sage*, 194.

Jesus and the Jewish religious leaders wished to spread holiness throughout the land, but they disagreed on procedure. The Pharisees wished to apply Levitical laws to everyday life of ordinary Jews, but the net effect of their program was to further divide and separate Jews from Samaritans, Gentiles, and others. Jesus by contrast stressed an intensification only of the basic moral demands of the Old Testament such as fidelity in marriage, honoring parents, and loving neighbor, coupled with a benign neglect or outright dismissal of the more divisive of the ritual requirements. The net result was conflict over holiness between Jesus and the Pharisees.

Perhaps what the passage represents is an apologetic for the scandalous behavior of Jesus and his disciples, who broke Levitical laws by associating with tax collectors and sinners. The Pharisees, together with "priests and Levites," would have viewed Jesus and his followers as ritually unclean and therefore, like the Samaritan, outcasts (see John 8:48). Jesus seems to be asking, not "who is my neighbor?" (Luke's editorial question in 10:29) but "how is one a neighbor?" If that is Jesus' primary concern in this passage, then his answer to the question is not "show compassion," but "demonstrate lavish compassion." As we know, the Samaritan not only acts compassionately, he becomes personally involved in the restoration of the victim, seeing him through to full health and well-being.

The parable, then, is eschatological at its core, for it teaches that when God's kingdom breaks into human lives and situations, it results in shocking patterns of behavior, where old prejudices die and new ways of life emerge. In this case Jesus is not relinquishing but rather intensifying the basic moral demands of Torah, exemplifying fully what it means to love one's neighbor. For Jesus, compassion trumps ritual holiness as a weightier matter of the law.

The primary purpose of this and other parables is not simply to instruct, but more importantly to move the listener/reader to decision or action. As a sage, Jesus taught to persuade, but never to coerce. Furthermore, he taught more by example than by prescription. His supreme achievement as a teacher was that he exemplified in himself all that he taught.

The Presence of the Kingdom in Luke's Gospel (Luke 13:10—19:27)

At the heart of Luke's Sermon on the Plain we find these words: "strive for [God's] kingdom" (Luke 12:31). According to this teaching, the kingdom is to be the believer's first and main concern. It was certainly so for Jesus, who gave up everything for the sake of the kingdom. The theology of Jesus does not admit compromise; there must be a complete break with conventional morality or piety. For example, a rich young man is told by Jesus that he must sell all that he has and give to the poor (Luke 18:18–30). To understand the meaning of such severity, this story must be read contextually. Jesus is on his way to Jerusalem, and the final conflict in which he is to be engaged looms before him. At such a time there can be no hesitation; it must be all or nothing. This is a moment of crisis for those who would follow Jesus. In Luke's travel narrative, when Jesus says, "You cannot serve God or wealth" (Luke 16:13), he is not giving a new commandment. He is simply stating a fact about the choices his followers must make. Before them lie two mutually exclusive worlds. Those who choose to live in one are automatically excluded from the other. When money has priority, God's lordship is compromised: "No one who puts a hand to the plow and looks back is fit for the kingdom of God" (Luke 9:62).

In a related passage, the parable of the Rich Fool (Luke 12:16–21), Jesus responds to a request to settle a dispute. Inheritance laws indicated that the eldest son should receive a double portion (Deut 21:15–17), but whatever the specifics of the dispute, Jesus redirects the focus, warning about greed. Considered a mark of depravity and the origin of other sins, greed was a common subject of moral instruction in the Jewish and the Greco-Roman world. While some interpreters view this parable as a metaphor about the kingdom, it can be said to pertain to the kingdom only in its implication of what kingdom living might mean with regards to one's focus or mindset regarding priorities and the use of resources.

If this parable is an example story, the rich man is a negative example of a person who foolishly trusts in possessions, including the resources of his or her mindset, and who misses life (both abundant life and eternal life) by presuming that possessions are life. In the end, the parable is about the relation of life to death, suggesting that those who live for worldly possessions and pursuits are already in a state of spiritual death. Nevertheless, the real issue of the parable is the meaning of life. Wisdom consists in striving for God's kingdom (Luke 12:31). However, like the fool in Psalm 14:1, the rich man leaves God out of the picture, seeking security in possessions.

The parable thus functions as a commentary on the second half of Luke 12:15, "for one's life does not consist in the abundance of possession." Spirituality is not opposed to wealth, but warns against thinking that

Jesus' Use of Parables

possessions are life. It is true that Jesus tells the rich young ruler to "sell all" and follow (Luke 18:22), but he is there prescribing an individual remedy and not a universal rule. Wealth can be beneficial when shared with others, but the meaning of this parable is that satisfaction from possessions is temporary and ultimately illusory. The fault is not in possessions themselves, but in how tightly we cling to them or the use we make of them (or refuse to make of them). This parable, unique to Luke's gospel, opposes the idolatry of security and urges a profound trust in God. Jesus ends the parable in a terse sentence that sharply draws the line between the "within" and "without" of our lives. We must choose, he says, between mundane treasure and being "rich toward God."

In Luke 14:26–27, Jesus is quoted as saying: "Whoever comes to me and does not hate father and mother, wife and children, brothers and sisters, yes, and even life itself, cannot be my disciple." These powerful and troublesome lines, their rhetoric softened in the Matthean parallel (see Matt 10:37–38), were not intended to be taken literally (see Mark 7:9–13). As noted earlier, they are an example of Middle Eastern hyperbole, so common in the gospels. Luke's audience was comfortable with extremes—light and darkness, truth and falsehood, love and hate—primary colors with no grey tones or hints of compromise. To say, "I like this and hate that" means "I prefer this to that." For the followers of Jesus, to hate their families meant to give them second place in their affection. However, as the reference to carrying one's cross in 14:27 indicates, there is a cost to discipleship, and that cost often implies relationships, as Paul notes in 2 Corinthians 6:14–16.

These are radical sayings. It is quite plain that if everyone gave away all their possessions to the poor, the only result would be that the rich of today would become the poor of tomorrow and vice versa; the social situation would be neither changed nor improved. Not every command is of equal application to every situation; there must be a measure of adaptation and flexibility. But before we become too easily dismissive of Jesus' radicalism, let us remember that Christian ethics are derived from Christian theology. The central point of that theology is the example of Jesus Christ and his demand that citizens of the kingdom recognize unconditionally the sovereignty of God.

In Luke 13:29 the kingdom of God is shown as a great gathering that includes all humanity. In Luke's version, the gathering takes place from the four points of the compass. This image, like the four-sided cross, is symbolic of the mystery of the kingdom, since its structure suggests the wholeness and harmony of God's kingdom. Its breadth and length, height and depth, embrace what is on the right and left and unite all in Christ, the center. In Ephesians 2:14–16, the reference is to the union, through Christ, of Jew and Gentile, but the image also applies to the union of our personality, the sensual and the intuitive, the spirit and the flesh, the inner and the outward, the knowable and the unknowable, logic and imagination, darkness and light.

We must always remember that the context of Jesus' sayings was the message that God's kingdom was near at hand. Jesus' claims placed persons on the very borderline between the old age and the new. Jesus' perspective made love, not duty, central. However, such love is no natural sentiment or calculated act but is patterned after the love of God. As God's love is bestowed unconditionally upon those least deserving to be loved, so likewise Christians must love even those who seem to be most loveless, including social outcasts or despised enemies. Jesus transforms religious laws by destroying legalism: Christ is the "end of the law" (Rom 10:4). Rather than setting a standard of perfection that drives us to despair, Christ teachings provide a compass that gives direction to our efforts to improve and transform society. Christian ethics, then, are essentially "resurrection ethics," since they derive their motive and patterns from the love of God manifested in Christ: "Beloved, since God loved us so much, we also ought to love one another" (1 John 4:11).

Despite the emphasis on the present nature of the kingdom, the New Testament also looks forward to the End, to the time when the last enemy has been overthrown and God's absolute sovereignty is established with finality. Thus the expression in the Lord's Prayer: "Your kingdom come" has both a present and a future element, for while it has to do with daily realities, it looks forward to the end of evil on earth, when God's sovereignty is unopposed.

For Jesus, parables are narrated answers to the question, "What is the kingdom of God like?" Luke's travel narrative contains several intriguing parables. In addition to the Mustard Seed (13:18–19) and the Yeast (13:20–21), which speak of the kingdom as present in germinal and dynamic form, Luke 15 narrates three parables of God's mercy: the Lost Sheep (15:4–7), the Lost Coin (15:8–10), and the story of the Lost Sons, known as the parable of the Prodigal Son (15:11–32). These parables teach about mercy and forgiveness, about God's persistence in seeking what is lost. To call people "lost" is to pay them a compliment, for it means that they are precious in the sight of God. Like God, we, too, should be jubilant when someone's search is successful, when one who is lost is found.

Jesus' Use of Parables

The specific use of the number 100 in the parable of the Lost Sheep is significant. In biblical times, the number 10, with its multiples of 100 or 1000, was considered perfect or complete. That is why the loss of just one sheep is so important, why one sheep must be found or the one hundred will not be complete. One might as well end up with thirty-seven or forty-five as with ninety-nine as far as completeness is concerned. This also explains the great joy over having found the one lost sheep.

A similar meaning belongs to the parable of the Lost Coin, which in Greek is about ten drachmas. A drachma is worth about six cents, so it is not a valuable coin. Yet the woman who has lost this coin goes to great efforts to find it because in the Eastern world, a woman was given ten coins by her husband at the time of their betrothal as a pledge of love and loyalty. These coins she was to retain all her life. To lose one was a terrible disgrace and an ominous portent for the marriage. This explains why the woman went to such lengths to find the lost coin and why she called together her friends to celebrate her recovery of the lost piece. We see again the symbolism of completion. As far as their symbolic value is concerned, one might as well lose eight or nine of the coins as to lose one of them.

As Luke 15:11 makes clear, the parable of the Prodigal Son is a story about two sons, both of whom are lost to their father, one in a foreign country, the other to self-righteousness. Both brothers were selfish, though in totally different ways. The selfishness of the younger brother was a reckless love of life, that of the elder to duty. While the elder was devoted to his father's service, never disobeying the rules of society, yet he was the center of his world, unable to enter sympathetically into the joys and sorrows of others. When he hears the merriment caused by the prodigal's return, his impulse is not to join in the revelry but rather to ask for an explanation. The news of his brother's return sets him thinking of his own rights and entitlements, jealously supposing himself to be wronged because his wayward brother is treated with more than justice. He disowns his brother, calling him "this son of yours," painting him in the worst light possible. The father refuses to take sides; with all their shortcomings he loves them both and never ceases to regard them as sons. The moment of redemption occurs when the younger brother "came to himself," or, as the King James Version states, "came to his senses," that is, confronted himself and his one-sidedness. This self-confrontation must also occur with the older brother.

The parable was told not to offer a generous pardon to the nation's delinquents, but to entreat respectable Jews to rejoice with God over the restoration of sinners, and to warn them that until they learned to do this, they would remain estranged from their heavenly father and pitifully ignorant of God's true character.

In this gospel, Luke records numerous stories that have something to do with Jesus sitting at a table. Luke 14 focuses on eating and table-fellowship. The chapter begins with Jesus going for a meal to the house of one of the leading Pharisees. Luke notes that the guests watch Jesus closely. In that hostile setting, Jesus tells three short stories: (1) choosing places at table (14:7–11); (2) choosing guests (14:12–14); and (3) invited guests who make excuses (14:15–24).

For Luke, the table is the place of fellowship and communion. It is also the place where Jesus redefines the social order by doing things differently and challenging those who are in control of the social order—the rich, the elders, the scribes, and the "politically correct." For Luke, the theme of table fellowship seems to be Jesus' unique form of visual sermon, cultural critique, and social protest. When you have a party, Jesus says, "invite the poor, the crippled, the lame, and the blind" (14:13). As Jesus implies, the new order of the kingdom will not simply ignore the status symbols of the world, but reverse them. Human hierarchies mean nothing to God. What matters is our common humanity and the desire to be in fellowship. In his parables and stories, Jesus is empowering the outsider. The apostle Paul also implemented this message in his churches when he declared, in one of his most revolutionary statements: "There is no longer Jew or Greek . . . slave or free . . . male and female; for you are one in Christ Jesus" (Gal 3:28).

In 14:33 Luke addresses the renunciation of possessions, an issue that resurfaces often in his writing, as it does in 18:18–30, in the idyllic summaries in Acts 2:44–45 and 4:32–37, as well as in the instructive story of Ananias and Sapphira in 5:1–11.

Among the Jewish people of Jesus' day, wealth was thought of as a sign of God's blessing. Jesus disagreed. Despite the wealth and prosperity gospel many preachers are proclaiming nowadays, power and success are not signs of God's blessing. "It is easier for a camel to go through the eye of a needle," Jesus noted, "than for someone who is rich to enter the kingdom of God" (18:25). Of course, we must not read this as an absolute law, or seek its enforcement, for that is not what Jesus was teaching. He was simply answering a question, discerning insincerity in the ruler's query. He seems to be saying, "If you want to enter into the freedom I am talking about, if you want to live authentically, here's my answer: Give it away. It will possess you more than you will ever possess it." When the man replies, "I am not ready to live like that," Jesus replies, "Okay, you asked, I answered."

If Americans were to select one book of the Bible and say, "This is going to be our guidebook, our philosophy of life," I doubt it would be Luke's gospel, because it hits us too deeply in areas where most are quite comfortable. Luke punctuates his discussion on wealth and discipleship with an impossible one-liner: "none of you can become my disciple if you do not give up all your possessions" (14:33).

Luke 16 forms a distinct unit that begins and ends with a parable—the Dishonest Steward and the Rich Man and Lazarus—each of which begins, "There was a rich man." Between the two is a collection of sayings that were addressed to "the Pharisees, who were lovers of money" (16:14). The warning that one's wealth must be handled wisely is a recurring theme in Luke's travel narrative. Following a section on the coming of God's kingdom (17:20-37), and two parables in 18:1-14 (namely, the parable of the Unjust Judge in 18:1-9 and the parable of the Pharisee and the Tax Collector in 18:9-14, in which Jesus calls a person righteous who was known to be unrighteous and refuses this description for a person whom everyone would recognize as righteous), in 18:15 Luke returns again to Mark's gospel, which he has not used since 9:30. He takes over with slight alteration the two stories of the children and the rich man, which Mark had placed side by side because together they describe the conditions of entry into the kingdom of God. The story of the blessing of the children is a rebuke to that adult complacency that regards children as beneath the notice of God. It assures us that children (even infants, according to Luke) whose parents bring them to God in faith belong already to God's family and therefore to God's kingdom (this theme, important to the synoptic tradition, also appears in 10:21 and 17:2) Let us be clear, however; Jesus is not asking his disciples to become childish. He commends to them only certain characteristics of childhood, including receptivity—meaning the ability to accept freely what is given—and teachability—the ability to learn and remain open to new and different things.

By contrast with the children, Luke's rich ruler (18:18-25) wished for nothing he could not earn. He supposed that entry into the kingdom was through effort and by accomplishment. He had passed "Intro to Religion 101" to his own satisfaction, and now wished to attempt "Advanced Religion 402." Jesus' response is unexpected: entry into eternal life is a miracle of God's grace, which cannot be earned but only accepted with humility and faith. The peril of possessions is that they stand in the way of this redeeming grace.

The long period of journeying toward Jerusalem, which began at Luke 9:51, draws to its close in 18:35. The parable of the Pounds (19:11–27), which Jesus tells as he nears Jerusalem, is given as a warning to those who misunderstand his coming to Jerusalem. In light of the passion prediction in 18:31–34 and the ignorance of the disciples in 18:35 ("But they understood nothing about all these things"), the parable is probably directed to the clueless disciples. The misguided expectation of the disciples is clarified in Matthew's gospel, where after his encounter with the ruler, Jesus informs his disciples that "after the renewal of all things, when the Son of Man is seated on the throne of his glory, you who have followed me will also sit on twelve thrones, judging the tribes of Israel" (Matt 19:28). Mark's gospel does not include this reference and Luke waits until a more opportune moment, as part of the instructions given at the Last Supper, to include it. For the disciples, the consummation of the kingdom was imminent, somehow connected with their journey to Jerusalem.

Throughout the early church there were many who expected an imminent return of Christ, that he would return in glory within a generation. When the first generation had passed, it was natural that there should be some reappraisal of the eschatological hope. Matthew emphasizes the future coming of the kingdom, but Luke adopts a different understanding. He gives prominence to sayings in which the kingdom is a present reality, and tones down the futuristic note in others (9:27; 22:69; see Mark 9:1; 14:62). In Luke's view, the imminent crisis predicted by Jesus was his own death, involving persecution for his followers and judgment for Jerusalem. The final crisis of history would be sudden, but might be indefinitely delayed.

Questions for Discussion and Reflection

Having read chapter 10, answer the following questions, writing your answers in a journal. If you are in a group study, be prepared to share your answers with those in the group.

1. In interpreting parables and other biblical passages, should modern readers focus on their original meaning and setting (on what the passage *meant*), or on what such passages might mean in our lives and time? If you opt for the latter, most modern interpreters follow certain

Jesus' Use of Parables

guidelines or institute boundaries as safeguards to prevent purely wishful, subjective, or arbitrary interpretations. In your case, what or whose guidelines should you follow?

2. Read Mark 4:10–12 and in your own words, explain your understanding of Jesus' use of parables.

3. Explain how Jesus' parable of the new wine in old wineskins in Luke 5:38–39 influences our understanding and interpretation of the gospel message, and by implication, Jesus' use of parables to convey his teaching.

4. After reading this chapter, explain the distinction between an "example story" (a traditional or narrative *mashal*) and a counter-order *mashal*. Examining the parable of the Good Samaritan contextually, do you believe Jesus wished his hearers to understand it as an example story or as a counter-order *mashal*? Explain your answer.

5. Have you ever been in a position where someone was mugged, beaten, or robbed? If so, what did you do? After reading the parable of the Good Samaritan, what would you do?

6. After reading this chapter, how can a contextual reading of Luke's parable of the Rich Man (18:18–30) help explain the radicality of its message and its eschatological (rather than its ethical) meaning?

7. After reading this chapter, how does an eschatological reading of the parables of Jesus (that is, how does affirming their connection to kingdom theology) influence their interpretation?

8. After reading this chapter, explain the nondualist implications in passages such as Luke 13:29.

9. After reading this chapter, explain the meaning of Romans 10:4 that Christ is the "end of the law."

10. After reading this chapter, explain how the three parables of "lostness" in Luke 15 describe the nature of God's kingdom.

11. From Luke's perspective, explain the benefits of "lostness." To what extent can we say that the elder brother in the parable of the Prodigal Son (Luke 15:11–32) was also "lost"?

12. After reading the segment on the Prodigal Son, explain the meaning of the statement, "The selfishness of the younger brother was a reckless love of life, that of the elder to duty."

13. After reading the parable of the Prodigal Son, someone might say that it teaches that it is better to sin and repent than not to sin at all. What is your opinion? What guidance does Romans 6:1–4 give us?
14. After reading this chapter, explain the parabolic nature of eating and of table-fellowship in the gospel of Luke.
15. After reading this chapter, explain Jesus' perspective on wealth, prosperity, and possessions.

11

Matthew's Parables in Nondual Consciousness

THE CUSTOMARY APPROACH TAKEN to interpreting or understanding Jesus' parables, found so often in preaching and teaching, is to allegorize them, paraphrasing or retelling them as patterns or illustrations of how to live and act as Christians in an essentially hostile social and moral environment. This moralizing approach is not the one we take, for if attracting and entertaining a crowd is what Jesus intended, his audience would not have reacted with such astonishment and perplexity as they did, as Matthew indicates at the conclusion of the Sermon on the Mount ("Now when Jesus had finished saying these things, the crowds were astonished at his teaching"; 7:28) and of his segment on the parables of the kingdom in 13:54: "He came to his hometown and began to teach the people in their synagogue, so that they were astonished and said 'Where did this man get this wisdom?'"

Once you become aware of the radical and paradoxical nature of Jesus' teaching, and by implication, his parables as a lens by which we understand the rest of scripture, we cannot miss seeing it elsewhere. And when we do learn this new way or reading scripture, this element of reversal and subversiveness becomes a common thread in virtually all of Jesus' teaching. And its principal target is not self-righteous Pharisees, self-confident fundamentalists, or even the current political or social situation, but the egoic mind. In his teaching, Jesus is deliberately bent on short-circuiting that grasping, acquiring, clinging, comparing linear brain to open within us a whole new mode of perception (not *what* we see but *how* we see; how the mind makes its connections). This is a classic strategy of a master teacher of wisdom.

Parables of the Kingdom in Matthew 13

Following the lead of material presented in chapter 6 regarding the setting of Matthew's gospel as a community shaped by its training school for Jewish Christian scribes and by its understanding of Jesus as a master teacher, in this chapter we examine seven parables of Jesus found in Matthew 13, all termed parables of God's kingdom.[1] The list includes the parables of the Sower (13:3-8), the Wheat and the Weeds (13:24-30a), the Mustard Seed (13:31-32), the Yeast (13:33), the Hidden Treasure (13:44), the Precious Pearl (13:45), and the Dragnet (13:48), and two or arguably three allegorical interpretations, such as of the parable of the Sower (13:18-23), the Wheat and the Weeds (13:37-43), and the Dragnet (13:49-50).

Keeping in mind the Matthean community's scribal setting, it is quite possible that verses such as 13:9 and 30b as well as the allegorizing interpretations are editorial redactions or scribal interpolations. There is no question, however, that the kingdom announced by Jesus in Matthew's gospel is truly a kingdom, first and foremost in opposition to the current temporal kingdom in Palestine ruled by the Herodian dynasty and backed by a Roman emperor claiming divine authority and power. In addition, the harassed and beleaguered Matthean community, likely in or near Antioch in Syria, was further traumatized by a fractured relationship with its Jewish roots and now deprived of the relative security and wealth of the synagogue, more fully exposed to a seductive secular world saturated with Roman power.

In his teaching, Jesus appealed not only to his disciples, or even to the most select or intuitive among them, but also to large, diverse audiences. Therefore, his message had different levels of understanding. As we discover in the seven parables in Matthew 13, to peasants and merchants, including farmers, fishers, artisans, husbands, wives, and parents, Jesus spoke with familiarity about planting and harvesting, cooking and baking, fishing, and acquiring objects of value. This chapter pictures a world that is quite familiar to his audience, yet is also characterized by genuine

---

1. Some scholars find an eighth parable in this chapter, namely in 13:52, which functions as a metaparable or "parable of parables" in that it invites the hearer/reader to enter the parabolic process by creating new parables to add to the ones just given.

newness, for underlying his everyday world is a new way of living, thinking, and being. Receiving the fullness of God's gift for our lives—what Matthew calls "the kingdom of heaven"—requires diligence, determination, concern, knowledge, and risk-taking, but above all, insight and discernment. At the right time good gifts must be acquired and bad ones let go, for only then what God has given us will establish a world ruled by God.

As we learn from Jesus' parables in Matthew 13, particularly the parable of the Sower (13:3–8), the Wheat and the Weeds (13:24–30), and the Dragnet (13:47–48), this world, while good in principle, is beleaguered by enemies—primarily viewed as bad decisions caused by ignorance, arrogance, detachment, and self-concern. Hence what is needed is confidence, trust, wisdom, and vision to keep hope alive. This vision is lived out in caring for one's household in the best possible manner, as God cares for all of his people. This world holds many good things, treasures to be used intentionally and with purpose. In a world full of what may initially look like good possessions, we must distinguish carefully between gifts that nurture God's kingdom and factors that will ultimately threaten or spoil its goodness.

The first thing we notice in the parables of Matthew 13 is their practical nature. Two of the stories, that of the Sower and of the Wheat and the Weeds, are markedly realistic stories of agricultural life in Jesus' time. In view of this observation, it is safe to say that the greater part of Jesus' audience had direct experience of working in the fields and fishing in the Sea of Galilee. Thus, when Jesus was telling the crowd the story of the Sower, we can assume that the audience's attention would have been captured by familiar images of farm work and not by eschatological or theological images of the coming kingdom, or of existential or spiritual images of a need for a change in consciousness or awareness.

Nevertheless, support for this latter interpretation comes from the first word Jesus utters in this parable: "Listen!" calling the crowds into seeing what these parables will come to reveal. The Greek word translated "listen" in 13:3 is used here to convey a meaning similar to "perceive," "understand," or "see" and "hear" in 13:13, 14, 16, and 17, where the disciples are promised to see a new reality in the parables told by Jesus. Hence, already at this point the reader can assume that this newness is found in, and focuses on, the sower's work of planting, and likely not—as the allegorical interpretation of the parable does—on the different types of soil.

In a sermon on the parable of the Sower, Barbara Brown Taylor notes how initially she focused on the types of soil, worrying about the nature of the soil represented by her own life. Thinking of how many birds were in her spiritual field, how many rocks and thorns, she started to worry about how she could clean them all up, turning herself into a well-tilled, well-weeded, well-fertilized field for the sowing of God's word. But then she noticed something wrong with reading this parable as a call to improve her life. If the parable was about different kinds of soil, why had it been known for centuries as the parable of the Sower? Perhaps the story is not primarily about us at all, but about the sower? If so, then what we should focus on is the extravagance of a sower who does not seem to be fazed by concerns about obstacles and impediments, but rather about flinging seed everywhere, wasting it with holy abandon, a sower who keeps on sowing no matter the consequences, confident that there is enough seed to go around, and that when the harvest comes it will fill every barn in the neighborhood to the rafters.[2]

If the parable of the Sower focuses not on us and our shortfalls but on the generosity of our Maker, who does not obsess about the condition of the fields, who is not stingy with the seed but who casts it everywhere, on good soil and bad, who is not cautious or judgmental or even very practical, but who seems willing to keep reaching into his seed bag for all eternity, covering the whole creation with the fertile seed of his unconditional love, then the parable begins to sound quite new.

The parable of the Sower, one of the best-known of Jesus' parables, has a foundational role in all three synoptic gospels. It is the first substantive parable in all three and, other than Matthew's parables of the Wheat and the Weeds and of the Dragnet, is the only parable given a detailed interpretation. The parable of the Sower is given pride of place in each synoptic gospel at the beginning of crucial instruction on parables of the kingdom (Matthew 13, Mark 4, and Luke 8). This parable is *the* parable about parables.

If we read the parable from the existential and spiritual levels of consciousness, we can focus on the result of the sowing along a continuum, from abysmal failure and partial or temporary misunderstanding of dualistic levels of understanding to full perception in nondual consciousness. Or, better yet, we can focus on the Sower's unswerving nature and resolve and on the fact that the sowing continues whether well received or not. In the end, the farmer is rewarded with unimaginable success, for unconditional love always triumphs in the end.

---

2. Taylor, *Seeds of Heaven*, 25–26.

Matthew's Parables in Nondual Consciousness

In sum, the parable shows past and present readers a world in which in any given field there is enough good soil that, though admittedly not perfect, is truly sufficient. The world of the parable of the Sower has flowing through it a kingdom that is reminiscent of the primal paradise envisioned in Genesis 2:8–9, an inner garden each of us is responsible to "till and keep" (Gen 2:15). The seeds of wisdom, awareness, harmony, unity, and understanding sown by the Sower in this parable are truly gifts of God, whose gracious and steadfast nature results in gifts of abundance and joy.

Reading the parable of the Wheat and the Weeds in continuation with the parable of the Sower, we immediately notice a number of similarities as well as some significant changes.[3] The protagonist is still a sower, but unlike the earlier parable, this time the seed and not the soil is qualified as good, and at the onset of the story, the work of sowing has already been completed. Furthermore, though the landlord has many trusted servants, it is he who does the arduous work of sowing. Upon completion of the work, the members of the household sleep soundly, seemingly confident that everything will follow its natural course (in this regard, see Mark 4:26–29).

That such optimism proves wrong is realized when during the night an enemy of the estate trespasses upon the field and sows weeds among the wheat. The next morning the master's servants appear baffled. Did the master sow bad (contaminated) seeds? Knowing this to be wrong, the landowner explains to his servants that an enemy has done this. When the servants suggest that the best solution is to uproot the weeds, the master disagrees, explaining that this would harm the wheat as well. The solution is to allow both weeds and wheat to grow together until the harvest is gathered. At all costs the harvest must be protected in full, even by following a course of action that goes against usual practices.

In comparison to the world of the parable of the Sower, the story of the Wheat and the Weeds presents a more complex reality. In its first part, an almost ideal reality is sketched, in which the God-given earth truly cares for humanity. Like the account of creation in Genesis, this parable presents a wholesome world of prosperity, good intentions, and peaceful surroundings. Like the first human beings, every human is created in God's image, their True Self oriented toward God and in harmony with itself, God, others, and nature. Before long, enemies arise, and seemingly pristine beings lose their innocence, exchanging their True Selves for a False,

---

3. This parable is being recognized as Matthew's rewriting of Mark 4:26–29, the parable of the Growing Seed, the latter a parable without clear parallels in the other gospels.

egoic existence. What is to be done? Will God forcibly remove our free will, or will God honor our decisions and enable us to learn from our experience and restore our True Self one person at a time, one harvest at a time? Will God's creatures willingly turn from their temporary first half of life existence, characterized by a self-centered, dualistic consciousness, to their eternal unitive consciousness, progressing gradually from prepersonal, personal, and transpersonal levels of consciousness?

Among the many surprises in this parable is that neither the master nor the servants desire retribution. Would it not have been our natural reaction in this situation to see to it that justice was served, our enemy apprehended and brought to judgment? That would be the natural response of first half of life mindsets. However, the consciousness this parable works to ensure is that the members of the household of God not lose what is their greatest possession: love of God, ultimately translating into love of one's enemies.

The second most natural response of first half of life mindsets is to try immediately to undo the harm that was done to the field. Perhaps some wheat might be damaged or destroyed by weeding, but this seems to be the price to be paid for a pure, spotless field. The master, however, decides otherwise. Every plant is valuable, no matter its condition, and no good plant must be threatened or damaged in the process. This leaves only one thing to do, to wait until harvest time and not, we might add, some future cosmic day of retribution, but a harvesting process that is ongoing and appropriate to each individual.

At the end of the parable[4] the pristine world pictured at the beginning of the story is restored. Despite the enemy's intrusion and the ill effects of the harmful occurrence, God's world has not been permanently tarnished. What could have turned into a world of retribution and revenge, or become a quest for a pure and spotless field, remains a world in which the harvest of all God's creatures remains the ultimate concern. Like the parable of the Prodigal Son in Luke 15:32, the lost son came to nondual awareness in remembering how well his father cares for all members of his household (Luke 15:17).

The five remaining parables of the kingdom in Matthew 13 are all relatively brief in nature and, while different in plot and setting, all reveal

---

4. According to biblical scholars, the original parable of Jesus likely ended in 13:30a, with the statement, "Let both of them grow until the harvest." The rest of the ending seems to be redacted, either by the author or by the Matthean scribal editor.

similar understanding of the "secrets" or "mysteries" of God's kingdom (that is, of the nature of God's will, rule, or plan of salvation). According to Matthew 13, the kingdom is present in Jesus but not yet fully consummated. In the parable of the Sower, we discover that the kingdom of God is extravagant and ongoing, and that God is not dissuaded by partial success or even by seeming failure. In the parable of the Wheat and the Weeds, we learn that God is tenacious, sowing good seed despite opposition, and not bent on revenge or retribution.

In the parable of the Mustard Seed (Matt 13:31–32), we learn that the kingdom, which one day will be a great tree, is already present in seed form. It might seem small, insignificant, and irrelevant, but by virtue of faith it will grow into a large fruitful tree. Already at this point in the study of Jesus' parables we become aware that seen together, these are not isolated stories, revealing scattered information about God's kingdom, but are stories intertwined and interconnected into an increasingly more meaningful and complete image of what the kingdom of God is like, and what this world, for that reason, ought to be. The kingdom of God is a realm (or a form of consciousness) in which a field that is only partially receptive, spoiled with weed, and in which only one seemingly very small seed is planted (our True Self), against all odds and in defiance of disasters and harmful deeds of enemies brings forth an astonishing yield.

The parable of the Yeast (Matt 13:33) consists of a single sentence picturing the kingdom of God as leaven (our True Self) that is taken by a woman and is evenly dispersed within the dough in such a way that the whole of it is leavened. Akin to all protagonists of the previous parables in Matthew 13, the kneading woman does not end her work until all of the flour (all human nature) is leavened. According to this parable, the kingdom of God, which one day will rule the world, enters the world in a form that is hardly perceptible. Contrary to first-century Jewish expectation (and much ongoing Christian expectation) of a military, political, and religious kingdom, according to Jesus' teaching, God's kingdom comes in an unexpected way, in a way that could easily be overlooked or even despised.

The next two parables in Matthew 13 liken the kingdom of God to a treasure hidden in a field (13:44) or to a pearl of great value that a merchant buys by selling all he has (13:45). While it is easy to allegorize the images of the hidden treasure and the pearl as standing for a heavenly reality or an earthly reality such as the land of Israel or nature in general, our interpretation of these images, building on the themes of seed, field, harvest, and flour in the preceding parables, focuses on inner spirituality, levels of consciousness, and the discovery of aspects associated with second half life thinking, living, and being.

The discovery of the treasure that is found and surprisingly hidden once again causes the finder to rejoice in a way that expresses deep satisfaction and great inner joy. However, different from what might be suspected from someone who suddenly comes to riches, the finder does not boast with his discovery but prudently invests in the source of the treasure. Having truly recognized its value, he sells everything he has to purchase the field. Likewise, the merchant who finds the precious pearl sells everything he has and buys this one fine pearl. Although the protagonist of this parable is an established merchant (or skilled philosopher, teacher, pastor, or theologian), he or she remains open to new awareness. Recognizing the value of unitive consciousness, the seeker risks all relative prosperity to acquire it. Thus, as in Matthew 6:21 and 33, we are to strive first for God's kingdom, for where our treasure is, there our heart will be also.

The parable of the Dragnet (Matt 13:47–48), like that of the Pearl, begins with the word "again," thereby aligning itself with the two parables preceding it. Setting aside 13:49–50 as editorial additions not likely included in Jesus' original parable, the imagery of this parable refers to work common and well known to all people living at or near the Sea of Galilee. Speaking of an act practiced by most who fished in the lake, a dragnet thrown into the water would gather various species of fish. After pulling it ashore, fishers would separate the good fish from bad and inedible ones. The good fish intended for consumption would be gathered and be brought to the market at once, while the poorer or spoiled ones would be discarded.

Like the contents of the dragnet, the spiritual world is a word filled with challenges, in which its fruit, given by God, must be used wisely and prudently according to their nature. Moreover, the world shown in these parables is a world that calls for decision. Not all that is gained is of equal value. At the right time, higher forms of consciousness must be separated from inferior ones and discarded. This can only be accomplished through discernment, grace, and by following our heart's lead. When our heart is ready, we will know. Likewise, the community created by God's kingdom in this world is not a pure community. Its citizens are called to be faithful to their True Self, and it is God who does the harvesting. What is remarkable in the spiritual world is that the harvest will yield an abundant catch, filling God's net.

As in the Wheat and the Weeds, there are lower and higher levels of consciousness within us all, and like adept fishers, spiritual seekers must seek the higher levels while discarding the lower ones. If our spiritual seeing and hearing are healthy, our whole body will be full of light, but if our seeing and hearing are unhealthy, our whole body will be full of darkness (see Matt 6:22–23). To paraphrase Matthew 6:24–25, just as a person cannot serve two masters, so we cannot be devoted to two levels of spiritual consciousness. If the seed planted by the Sower is good, and if the land is fertile, the yield will be extraordinary.

Parables of Joy and Rejoicing in Matthew 18–22

In this segment we examine six parables of Jesus found in Matthew's gospel: the Lost Sheep (18:12–14), the Unforgiving Servant (18:23–34), the Two Sons (21:28–31a), the Wedding Banquet (22:1–13), the Talents (25:14–30), and the Sheep and the Goats (25:31–46). Continuing the line of reasoning set forth to this point, the material in these parables continues to develop the image of the kingdom of God and of the need for a higher (nondual and unitive) level of consciousness in a number of significant ways.

First, the interconnectedness of the real and ideal worlds pictured in the parables of Matthew 13 increasingly gains complexity and demands from the reader a high level of awareness. Second, the various characters shown in the parables take on very different roles in view of working for or against the realization of God's will on earth. Contemplating the practices that flow from the action in the parables requires sharp discernment of which actions exposed in the parables should be followed and imitated and which must be identified as detrimental to living, thinking, and being in God's new kingdom. As we note in the exposition of the parable of the Two Sons, all readers of the parables are called to arrive at a true change of heart (see the important word *metanoia* in Matthew 3:2, traditionally translated as "repent" but literally meaning a change of mind or heart, to be followed by immediate action). The repentance that Jesus talks about means "to go beyond the mind" or "to go into the large mind," signifying that his followers are to go beyond their small egoic operating systems that declare, "I think, therefore I am," into a larger unitive operating system that acknowledges, "I am, therefore I think." And it is Jesus, the master of repentance, who leads us there.

In the end, the picture we get from these parables is characterized by the immense joy of imitating and implementing the will of God through our nondual action here on earth. Although by the dualistic standards of the real world nondual consciousness could be judged careless, reckless, foolish, and even unjust, in the last resort such consciousness transcends the principles and expectations of the real world, with the single intention of bringing salvation to the repentant.

Found in the gospels of Matthew and Luke, the parable of the Lost Sheep holds a vital place in Matthew and, according to the introductory statement in 18:1, clearly sketches a genuine image of the kingdom of God. Given the context of children and child-like behavior and of the comment in 18:12 that a sheep has "gone astray," it is quite possible that the lost sheep had wandered unintentionally from the flock, and that in a careless moment, had seemingly wandered off in search of good grass and thus, when all the other sheep had moved on, following the call of the shepherd, had found itself lost and alone.

In childhood, adolescence, and even into one's adulthood, it is quite natural to follow the demands of one's False Self and only later, to discover its negative and misleading consequences. As with the parables of Matthew 13, the most conventional interpretation of this parable focuses on two aspects of the story. First, viewing the lost and found sheep as standing for the repentant members of the Christian community (see Luke 15:7), and second, viewing the shepherd as God and/or Christ (see Matt 18:14).

It is clear from Matthew's account that God cares for each member of the flock, particularly for those most innocent, defenseless, or in precarious positions, both morally and existentially. Realizing his loss, the shepherd immediately leaves the rest of the flock behind, thereby contravening common sense and practice. Literally abandoning his flock, the shepherd searches for the single lost sheep, and in finding that sheep, experiences true joy and bliss. Like the parable of the Prodigal Son, the father rejoices by proclaiming, "This son of mine was dead and is alive again; he was lost and is found!" (Luke 15:24). Such is the joy in God's kingdom when a person comes back to unitive consciousness, to his or her True Self. The parable of the Lost Sheep turns the potential tragedy of lostness into the joy of reuniting the lost sheep with the rest of the herd. Only in this way, the parable tells, can the true joy promised in the kingdom of God be experienced and lived here and now.

Matthew's Parables in Nondual Consciousness

The sheep was lost because it was out of touch—with its own vulnerability and with its precarious situation. Oblivious to its condition, it had become unaware that it was lost. It had become so independent and unattached that over time it failed to hear the voice of the shepherd calling. In this parable, Jesus tells us that God is always seeking those who are lost, always attuned to the cry of anguish of the sheep that is lost. God cares for the flock and knows each sheep intimately, so much so that like the Good Shepherd in John 10:3, calls each sheep by name—and the sheep know and hear the shepherd's voice, for they have an innate ear and voice by which they can share intimacy with their master.

Similar to the parable of the Sower, which begins with Jesus asking his disciples to open their eyes and ears to a new way of seeing and hearing, the parable of the Lost Sheep begins with the rhetorical question, "What do you think?" Like in the parable of the Two Sons (see Matt 21:28), Jesus is not expecting an intellectual understanding or response. In these parables, the question conveys a function similar to "listen" or "to see or perceive" in Matthew 13. Here thinking means to open one's eyes to gain a deeper insight and understanding of the reality described in the parable and its consequences for one's spirituality.

The final point Jesus relates in this parable is the will of God that no sheep in the flock be lost. While the last word in the parable is often translated as "lost," a better translation is "perish" or "be destroyed" (see Matt 2:13). This pronouncement of Jesus points to the fact that losing one sheep is not simply being left with a smaller herd. Losing a sheep means spiritual loss, destruction, and death, something unacceptable to God. Since no sheep must wander off and die, each lost sheep must be searched for and found at any cost.

This parable introduces the reader to perhaps the most important promise of God's kingdom, that abundant life—life in its fullness—is intended for, and must be guaranteed without discrimination, to all those in God's care (see Matt 24:14; John 10:10; Rom 8:37–39; Ps 23:1–6; 139:7–8). This promise is also instruction and command of how to live and act in God's kingdom. The joy of the shepherd is not simple elation or happiness for having restored what was lost, but the joy that God grants all who awaken to unitive consciousness.

At the outset the picture in this parable is an ideal world of blessing, like the garden of bliss described in Genesis 2. This ideal world features a shepherd in possession of a large number of sheep. Soon, however, this ideal world (our True Self) turns into the well-known real world (our False Self), in which "all we like sheep go astray" (Isa 53:6). When paradise seems irretrievably lost, the shepherd's actions are a gamechanger, for faced with the loss of even one sheep, he leaves all else to rescue his straying creature. In the spiritual world, it is not the survival of the fittest that matters, but mercy and grace that translate into salvation for all. Furthermore, God's risk-taking action—always sowing, always seeking—brings us to awareness of our lostness, and it is God's action of sowing and seeking that lead us back home. To this end, it might be appropriate to call this parable not simply the parable of the Lost Sheep, but the parable of Joy in Salvation.

Before examining the parable of the Two Sons (Matt 21:28–31a), I take a moment to comment on the enigmatic parable of the Unforgiving Servant in Matthew 18:23–34. The problem with this parable is that the king is both attractive as a magnanimous figure yet problematic in that he can renege on his forgiveness and send his servant to be tortured (18:34–35). Is God like or not like the king in this parable? This is the problem Christians encounter when they wrestle with the question whether God's mercy is trumped by God's judgment. Will we be judged according to wrath or according to mercy (see Rom 2:6 and Eph 2:8–9)?

Part of the value in this parable is in what it demonstrates about interpreting parables. According to biblical scholar Klyne Snodgrass, we must be careful not to read parables as if they were equation or as systematic theologies. Parables should be interpreted as analogies and not theologies, as analogies "that show *pieces* of reality but may contain other elements for a variety of purposes."[5] Parables are theological, but they must be allowed to do what they intend and not be pushed beyond their intentions. There is always an "is" and an "is not" to metaphors, and we ruin a parable if we forget the "is not" character of a metaphor.

For its many problems and paradoxes, an easy solution might be to say that this parable makes only one point, but such an approach would strip it of much of its value. Other interpreters, uncomfortable with the parable's depiction of the king as a figure for God, conclude that the king in the parable is intended to portray what God is *not* like. According to Snodgrass, the parable was not intended to serve as an illustration of Jesus' teaching in 18:21–22. Matthew's use of "for this reason" in verse 23 picks up only part of the subject of forgiveness, the necessity to forgive.

---

5. Snodgrass, *Stories with Intent*, 71.

As in the parable of the Lost Sheep, which calls for the reader to imitate the action of the shepherd, so the parable of the Unforgiving Servant speaks of the unexpected mercy of the king in forgiving the one particular servant who owes him an unpayable large amount of money. If the kingdom of God is like this king, who forgives us an unpayable spiritual debt, then we, God's servants, ought to be merciful, compassionate, and forgiving. If, however, we act like the Unforgiving Servant, unwilling to act with compassion and forgive those in our debt, then, like the servant in the parable of the Talents (Matt 25:14–30) to whom the landlord entrusted one talent, if we fail to reflect God's goodness to others, even what we have (our blessings and gifts, including our unitive consciousness) will be taken from us and given to those who are willing to risk their identity and well-being in selfless love, compassion, kindness, and forgiveness with all around them, particularly with those in need. In the gospels, this lesson is clearly illustrated in the parable of the Sheep and the Goats (perhaps more aptly called the parable of Seeing Christ in the Least Other) in Matthew 25:31–46.

Properly speaking, this is neither a parable nor an allegory, but a description of divine judgment. However, it contains parabolic images with allegorical significance. Like Jesus' other parabolic teachings, this discourse is not about moralism. More than a guidebook, the New Testament tells what Christian character is, not what actions must be done in particular situations. Disciples of Jesus are those who refuse boundaries with regard to neighbor, even to the inclusion of enemies whom they embrace in love. This passage may not tell us *how* to love neighbor as self, but it empowers each person to determine what path of wisdom best expresses their understanding of discipleship.

When studying this parable, it is important to understand that the analogy of sheep and goats in 25:32 is based on the separation of right and left, not on the character or nature of goats. In ancient Palestine, both sheep and goats were valued and were pastured together. Nothing cultural prepares the reader for the strong condemnation of the goats. What is stressed is their placement with regards to the Son of Man. According to rabbinic tradition, both Gehenna and the Garden of Eden existed long before the world, the former on the left of God's throne and the latter on the right.

Following the line of thought regarding forgiveness in the parable of the Unforgiving Servant (Matt 18:23–34), the reader of scripture certainly needs to do more than try harder, for attitudes and actions that disseminate the meaning of God's forgiveness have to flow from genuine faith established in unitive consciousness. Initially, we must act like the king and forgive those who cannot accept or return our forgiveness. Then we must encourage those whose debts are forgiven to likewise release the loans of their debtors and not turn into unmerciful creditors. Finally, we must exercise true Christian forgiveness that supersedes any concept of retributive justice. At time such actions require whistle blowing, not to seek the punishment or embarrassment of the offenders, but their spiritual transformation. As a result of the grace we have received from an all-loving God, the household of the redeemed needs to commit to changing this harsh unforgiving world into an ideal world reminiscent of God's reign. We do so not through obligation or reward but through what might be called "paying forward forgiveness."

In Matthew's parable of the Talents (25:14–30), the key to the story is not so much the bold, adventurous risk-taking of the first two servants, though that action is important and commendable, but the role of the servant with one talent. His two fellow servants are sketched in strong lines as becomes their clear-cut character, but the person with one talent is painted with sharp detail, and as the story develops, he occupies the bold center of this picture. He is not a bad person, not drunken, wasteful, or lacking in a sense of responsibility. What he lacks is imagination, and he fails in courage. He does not see that his talent is important or necessary. However, in the kingdom of God (in the realm of spirituality), every person's gift is necessary, and the distinction between "great" wealth and talent and "small" becomes irrelevant and illusory.

In a political election, for example, each person's vote is equally important and necessary, and a single voice can turn the tide of opinion one way or another. In life, as in God's kingdom, the one-talent person is as vital as the ten- or five-talent person. In the spiritual as well as the natural world, following a hunch, pursuing an interest, inclination, or ability, can energize a great cause. Likewise, neglecting these impulses can be equally destructive of potential. Maintaining the status quo, fearing change, backing normalcy is the buried talent.

As noted earlier, the text of the short parable of the Two Sons (21:28–31a) commences with a call to a new way of seeing the reality of God in this world (for a parallel to the question, "What do you think?" compare Matthew 17:25). Like the parable of the Prodigal Son in Luke 15:11–32, this short narrative presents a father—perhaps a landowner—with two sons, whom he asks to work for him that very day in the vineyard. Surprisingly, the first son refuses to do so. However, upon reflection, sometime later he feels regret and shows remorse. Realizing what he has said and intended was wrong, he proceeds to work on his father's estate.

Next, the father asks his second son to take up work in the vineyard, to which the son responds positively yet deferentially. However, the surprise in the story is that despite this son's clear assertion to be willing to work in his father's vineyard, he does not go there. At the end of the parable, it becomes clear that it is the first son who does the father's will.

On the face of it, the parable is about *metanoia*. The truth is that both sons are imperfect in their response to the father's request. A truly good child would be expected to consent wholeheartedly with a parent's wish. Likewise, a good child will not just pay lip service to a parent but follow his or her wish, even if this implies hardship.

The Christian life is often like that, where words and actions are often far apart from one another (see the conclusion of the Sermon on the Mount in Matthew 7:21–27). Like the saying about inner spiritual quality or consciousness in Matthew 7:16–20, doing God's will is not simply fulfilled by passively obeying religious duties and commandments, but by bringing forth good fruit. As a good tree (a good character and spiritual consciousness) cannot bear bad fruit, so, unfortunately, a poor character and spiritual consciousness cannot bear good fruit. We will know our spiritual nature by its fruit (doing God's will). When we think, act, and live according to God's will, then our world and the lives of those around us will be transformed into the ideal world in which co-creators with God labor for the becoming of God's kingdom.

Matthew's parable of a king who invites guests to his son's Wedding Banquet (Matt 22:1–13) consists of two larger parts. The first eight verses picture the king's invitation to the customary guests, who out of various reasons disrespect the invitation, even to the point of mistreating and murdering the king's messengers (in this context, see also the parable of the Vineyard in Matthew 21:33–44, especially 21:35–39). In the second part of the parable (22:9–13)[6] the same king orders his servants to invite people, good and bad alike, from the streets. However, when the wedding hall fills with visitors, the king notices one guest who does not wear a wedding gown. When the person is asked for an explanation for this offence, he seems stunned and remains speechless, whereupon the guest is bound

---

6. Most scholars regard this second part as originally separate and independent from the parable in 22:1–13.

and thrown out into the darkness. The parable ends with an explanatory afterthought by the Matthean editor, the intent being, "All are called, but not all are chosen (or adequately prepared)."

While the parable has traditionally been interpreted as an allegory referring to the rejection of God's offer of salvation by Jews and other non-Christians, what if we read it as a portrayal of God's invitation to the second half of life and its nondual (unitive) level of consciousness? While initially the invitation is sent to the customary guests (traditional religious folk, particularly Christians with first half of life commitments, standards, boundaries, and mindsets), their refusal to accept the gift of growth and openness to progressive transformation leads to a universal invitation to nonreligious guests, who willingly accept. However, one guest slips in with a first half of life level of consciousness, clothed in egoic consciousness (False Self) masquerading as his or her True Self (unitive consciousness). Such ignorance, duplicitous and inappropriate, is not appropriate in God's kingdom. By implication, such a way of being, living, and thinking is ill suited in God's kingdom and self-judged as unprepared and not yet ready, returns the guest to his or her egoic way of being, living, and thinking, referred to as "outer darkness."

When dealing with harsh or vindictive language in scripture, such as found in prophetic or eschatological oracles of doom or as in passages concluding parables such as Matthew 25:30 and Luke 19:27, we must keep in mind its metaphorical or parabolic nature. Casting someone into outer darkness, as in 22:13 and elsewhere in Matthew such as 8:12 and 22:13, for all intents and purposes means separation from everything good, specifically God. Such language should be taken as a warning and not as describing Jesus' "theology." By this I do not mean, however, that the language is irrelevant. God's judgment is real, and not to be taken lightly. Nevertheless, as gospel readers know, rather than doing the slaughtering, Jesus is the one slaughtered.

What is important about the parable of the Wedding Banquet is that spirituality is not about religion, laws, commandments, obligations, and duties. Many of us, if asked, might think of kingdom life as a courtroom or judgment scene, when, according to scripture, it is described as a banquet, a feast, a party, a wedding, and a marriage feast. In the gospels, while some fifteen passages refer to kingdom life as a festive celebration, one parable, that of the Sheep and the Goats in Matthew 25:31–46, depicts a courtroom or judgment scene. And that's good. We need Matthew 25 because it makes it clear that the ultimate issue God takes into account is how we care for the poor and marginalized. The foundational idea in scripture is that relation to God is by necessity lived out in relation to humans, particularly those in need. A person cannot be a follower of Jesus and be void of compassion, which is at the heart of the gospel. Elsewhere, the good news of Jesus is an invitation to attend a banquet. Everyone is invited, and the only people who don't get in on the party are those who don't want to come. However, once in the banquet, we are to live, act, and think as God's people. And the only attire necessary is a new consciousness, given to all who enter the door boldly and wholeheartedly.

At the conclusion of the parable of the Wedding Banquet, we wonder what might have happened had the guest without festive dress admitted his carelessness and requested suitable clothing. Knowing the king, he would have welcomed the opportunity (see the story of Zacchaeus in Luke 19:10, which concludes with the statement, "For the Son of Man came to seek out and to save the lost"). One possibility is that the king would have provided the requisite garment (see Matt 6:28–33), asked his servants to do so, or asked the guests to share with the person in need (see Matt 25:36), for that is what kingdom people are expected to do. Who knows, maybe the guest in need is none other than the king in disguise (see Heb 13:2; Gen 18:2–15, 33).

Questions for Discussion and Reflection

Having read chapter 11, answer the following questions, writing your answers in a journal. If you are in a group study, be prepared to share your answers with those in the group.

1. According to one influential school of interpretation, Jesus' parables contain one central teaching and should not be allegorized. However, as we see in the gospels, notably in Matthew 13, numerous parables are allegorized, and in this chapter, the author often resorts to allegorization as well. In your estimation, is allegorizing the parables legitimate biblical interpretation? If so, what limits or boundaries would you impose on such practice?

2. Assess the merit of the author's attempt to feature levels of consciousness and the need to move from one's False Self to one's True Self as an important way to interpret many parables of Jesus, particularly parables of the kingdom.

3. After reading this chapter, what did you learn about the historical setting of the community that produced Matthew's gospel?

4. As far as possible, identify or list three or four "enemies" of the kingdom of God.

5. In reading and interpreting the parable of the Sower, what are the advantages and disadvantages of focusing on the types of soil rather than on the nature and actions of the Sower?

6. After reading this chapter, what did you learn about egoic consciousness?

7. After reading this chapter, what did you learn about nondual consciousness?

8. After reading the parables in this chapter, what surprises did you encounter?

9. If you were asked to clarify what is meant by the "secrets" or "mysteries" of God's kingdom (see Matt 13:11), what answer would you give (other than "I don't know" or "I pass")?

10. Of the parables we examined in Matthew's gospel, which is your favorite? Why?

11. Of the parables we examined in Matthew's gospel, which do you find most perplexing? Explain your answer.

12

Hard Teachings of Jesus

IN HIS INSIGHTFUL BOOK *Putting on the Mind of Christ*, lawyer Jim Marion makes the important suggestion that we understand Jesus' phrase "the kingdom of heaven" not as a reference to the place where we go when we die, or even to a new sociopolitical reality on earth that Christians or even God will bring about, but as a metaphor for a state of consciousness. Viewed this way, God's kingdom is not a place to which we go or even a place at all, but a way of looking at reality, a transformed awareness that literally turns this world into a different place. According to Marion, God's kingdom stands for what we have been calling "nondual or unitive consciousness." The hallmark of this awareness is that it sees no separation—not between God and humans nor between humans and other humans. Such an understanding, such a way of living, thinking, and being, is what the Bible calls "love," labeled by the apostle Paul as the greatest of all virtues (see 1 Cor 13:13) and as the fulfillment of God's law and will (see Rom 13:8–10).

Loving God and neighbor as oneself are indeed Jesus' two core teachings, underlying everything he said and did. When Jesus talked about this Oneness, he was not speaking of an equivalence of being or of eliminating distinction between God and humans or of one human from another. Rather, what he had in mind was a complete mutual indwelling, a concept we spoke of in chapter 4 under the terms interabiding and *perichoresis*.

While Jesus did claim that "the Father and I are one" (John 10:30)—a statement viewed as blasphemous if taken literally—he did not see this Oneness as an exclusive privilege but as something shared by all human beings. There is no separation between humans and God because of this mutual interabiding that expresses the indivisible reality of divine love. Humans flow into God—and God into us—because it is the nature of love to flow. And as we give ourselves into one another in this fashion, the vine and the branches—the whole and the part—live together in mutual, loving reciprocity; each belonging to the other and dependent on the other to show forth the fullness of love. That's Jesus' unitive vision of no separation between human and divine.

No separation between one human and another is an equally powerful concept—and equally challenging. One of the most familiar teachings of Jesus is "Love your neighbor as yourself." Our first thought in this regard might be, "Wow, this is hardly possible," and our next thought is likely, "This is going to require great effort." If that is our response, we are mistaken, for we are not reading or hearing correctly. We hear, "Love your neighbor as much as yourself," but what Jesus is saying is not "as much as" but "as," that is, we are to love others naturally and authentically, as an extension of ourselves, as a continuation of ourselves, for that is how we and our neighbor are connected—through interbeing. There are not two separated, competing individuals out there, one seeking to be better at the price of the other, or one extending charity to the other. Rather, there are two interconnected beings sharing one common love, both cells of the one great Life. As Jesus modeled for us, when two cells flow naturally into one another, experiencing that one Life from the inside, they discover that "laying down one's life for another" is not a loss of one's self but a vast expansion of it, because the indivisible reality of love is the only True Self.

In chapter 5 I introduced the concept of a *koan*, suggesting that parables may be read and interpreted as paradoxical or riddle-like stories intended to turn our egoic mind upside down and push us into new ways of seeing. About a half century ago, a few biblical scholars became aware of this subversive dimension to Jesus' parables. John Dominic Crossan was one of the first to write about it, followed by Bernard Brandon Scott, whose 1989 book *Hear Then the Parables* was widely popularized through its influence on Thomas Keating.

Traditional Christians tend to read the Bible as God's rulebook and view Jesus as a nice person setting an example of niceness for us to imitate. Many of his teachings, including some of his best-known parables, have a paradoxical, perplexing, almost unsettling quality. As we saw earlier, parables are a wisdom genre, belonging to *mashal*, the Jewish tradition of sacred poetry, stories, proverbs, riddles, and dialogues through which wisdom is conveyed. In the Hebrew scriptures (the Old Testament), *mashal* is sometimes associated with riddles or perplexing sayings (Ps 49:4; 78:2; Prov 1:6; Ezek 17:2). In some cases the meaning of a parable is deliberately obscured in order to force the reader or listener to thought, and this might be what lies behind Mark's superimposed view in 4:10–12. While it is true that Jesus' parables draw upon a familiar world, the familiar is regularly used in a new way.

For example, in the parable of the Good Samaritan, the most famous of Jesus' parables (it is found in all three synoptic gospels), if you stick to the surface, it sounds like an uplifting tale about an attractive do-gooder. However, what makes the parable confrontational is the fact that the customary tables are reversed, for in this parable the fellow who gets beat up is a Jew, and the one who does the rescuing is a Samaritan. The story is told to a Jewish audience, but in their eyes, there was no such thing as a "good" Samaritan. As far as they were concerned, Samaritans were pariahs, to be despised and kept at arm's length. So the subversion begins when the Jew becomes the victim, and the pariah becomes his rescuer. Lying below the surface are disturbing questions: "Do we really know what's good and what's bad?" "Who are the righteous and who are the not righteous?" Such questions challenge our binary minds, which are quick to judge and feel self-meritorious.

We find a similar challenge in the parable of the Prodigal Son (Luke 15:11–32). Again, this is a familiar story, until we stop to think that it is about two lost sons, not one. While we tend to identify with the older brother, who is indignant over the extravagant reception his rebellious brother has received, we find here the same point Jesus is making in the parable of the Laborers in the Vineyard (Matt 20:1–16) regarding a theology of punishment and of reversal. These parables are not about wrath of God but rather about God's goodness. Once again, our sense of, "This isn't fair!" becomes a textbook example of our egoic operating system at work. Through the older son, Jesus is asking us to look closely at that part in each of us that insists on keeping score, that can't let go into the generosity and blessedness of nondual consciousness and second half of life thinking, living, and being. The parable's concluding image—of the older son standing alone outside, refusing to join the party because he feels he has been slighted—is a vivid symbol of the way our egoic operating system holds us back from joining the dance of divine mercy in full swing around us. Those stuck in their ego simply can't hear the music.

Living Water

As we discover when we look closely at Jesus' parables, they are not sweet teachings about people doing nice things for other people. Rather, they challenge the basic structures, assumptions, and beliefs about ourselves that keep the binary mind firmly in place. The parables are intended to challenge us, to confuse and disturb us, possibly even to make us angry; their purpose is to make us look at ourselves more closely. And isn't this the ultimate purpose of scripture as well?

Sometimes Jesus takes the language of paradox and riddle so far that he leaves people simply scratching their heads. Perhaps the classic example is Jesus' encounter with Nicodemus in John 3:1–15, when this member of the Pharisees comes to Jesus by night to discuss the nature of the spiritual life. It is noteworthy that Jesus is here said to be speaking to a Jewish rabbi (in 3:10 he is called "*the* teacher of Israel," suggesting he is Israel's leading sage) who is likely a member of the Sanhedrin, the ruling body in Palestinian Judaism. The presence of "we" in 3:2 makes it clear that Nicodemus has a representative and therefore a legitimate point of view. Nicodemus is a type of the sympathetic Jewish seeker; he represents learned Jews, who are said to recognize Jesus as a teacher sent from God, yet still remain "in the dark." Unlike the common people, who believe in Jesus because of signs of healing (2:23), Jesus desires real disciples. As a theologian, Nicodemus is bound by tradition and religious perspective. So the author of John's gospel uses him as a foil, not so much speaking with him but through him to the readers of the gospel, for Nicodemus soon disappears as he came, into the darkness of the night.[1]

The discussion about birth and new birth begins at 3:3, and much has been made of the fact that *anōthen* can mean "above" as well as "anew." This double meaning is not only possible in Greek, it seems intentional. Jesus' expression is a deliberate challenge for Nicodemus to move beyond surface meanings to a deeper meaning. The intentional double meaning of *anōthen* must be kept in mind when reading this verse in order to discern Jesus' full meaning and the nature of Nicodemus's misunderstanding. When Jesus tells Nicodemus that he must be born again from above, Nicodemus is stunned.

"Wait a minute," he exclaims. "This doesn't make any sense. How can a man go back into his mother's womb and be born again? What is this man talking about?"

---

1. Nicodemus does not disappear altogether, however; see 7:50–52 and 19:38–42, where he reappears in a more positive light.

Hard Teachings of Jesus

Jesus doesn't make things easy. Instead, he throws Nicodemus a statement intended to destabilize him—essentially the Christian equivalent of the famous Zen *koan*, "What is the sound of one hand clapping?"

The notion of spiritual birth should not be dissociated from that of the kingdom of God, with which it is joined. Reference to the kingdom of God is rare in John (3:3, 5; see also 18:36), unlike the synoptics, where it is a frequent metaphor of eschatological newness. To connect "to be born *anōthen*" with kingdom of God references suggests that the new birth of which Jesus speaks is also an eschatological category. Nicodemus assumes Jesus is referring to another physical birth by the phrase "born anew," whereas Jesus is referring to a birth of a different sort, caused by the work of the Holy Spirit, God's eschatological gift to his followers. Nicodemus's incredulous response in 3:4 is part of the recurring pattern of misunderstanding followed by explanation in John's gospel. As an educated Jew, Nicodemus thinks of the kingdom of God as participation in the new order God would bring about at the end of history. He cannot believe that the transformation of an individual's character is a requirement for entrance into the kingdom and therefore is amazed by Jesus' explanation (3:7, 12).

Being born from above is further explained in 3:5, where it means being born "of water and Spirit." Christian readers detect a baptismal reference here, but the emphasis throughout is on birth through the Spirit. If water/baptism is so important for entering the kingdom, it is surprising that the rest of the discussion never mentions it again; the entire focus is on the work of the Spirit (3:8), the work of God (3:16–17), and the place of faith (3:15–16). The analogy between the mysterious wind and the sovereign work of the Spirit (3:8) becomes very strange if Spirit-birth is tied to baptism. While the expression "born of water and Spirit" is not found in the Old Testament, water and spirit appear in Ezekiel 36:25–27, where hope for the future is tied to spiritual rebirth, imagery that anticipates the vision of dry bones in Ezekiel 37:1–14.

Assuming that John 3:6 describes two births, one from flesh to flesh and the other from Spirit to spirit, some interpreters propose that "born of water and Spirit" in 3:5 similarly refers to two births, natural procreation and the other supernatural, birth by the Spirit. To support this view, "water" is taken as a reference to the amniotic fluid that breaks from the womb before childbirth. Such a view, attractive on many levels, cannot be substantiated from ancient records, for there are no ancient sources that picture natural birth as "from water." Furthermore, the Greek construction does not favor two births here but one, since we have but one preposition (*ek*) before "water and Spirit," meaning they refer to one and the same birth. Verses 7–8 make clear that John is speaking only of spiritual regeneration, not about a physical and a spiritual birth. The analogy here between "wind" and the work of the Spirit is apt not only because one can detect the presence of the wind or Spirit by their respective effects, but also because in this gospel *hearing*, not seeing, the Word is the prerequisite to new birth and entering the kingdom of God.

Once you catch the subversive edge in even the more familiar teachings of Jesus, it becomes easier to approach other parables, sayings, and teachings of Jesus that the church as a whole has never quite known how to deal with. They are scattered throughout the four gospels, but many appear in the passion narratives. One of the thorniest of these is the parable of the Wise and Foolish Bridesmaids in Matthew 25:1–13. As the story opens, a great wedding feast is about to take place, and the ten bridesmaids are waiting for the bridegroom to come. But he is delayed, and they all fall asleep. In the middle of the night they hear the cry, "The bridegroom is coming!" Five of them have remembered to bring oil for their lamps, so they light their lamps and head into the banquet hall. The other five haven't brought spare oil, and their lamps are now out of fuel. They ask the five "wise" bridesmaids, "Can we borrow some of your oil so that we can go in to the wedding feast as well?" But the five refuse, saying if they share, there won't be enough for them. "Go to the dealers and buy some for yourselves." While the foolish bridesmaids head for the merchants, the bridegroom arrives, and together with the wise maidens who were ready and prepared to meet him, enter the banquet hall to celebrate the wedding. While the foolish maidens are purchasing oil, the doors of the hall are shut for the night, and the foolish maidens find themselves locked out.

While we often hear that the point of the parable is the importance of watchfulness, then none of the bridesmaids were successful, for all fell asleep. In its literary context, namely, Matthew's eschatological discourse (chapters 24–25), the point is the delay of the bridegroom, arguably a reference to the delay of the kingdom of God or the eschatological return of Christ, and the need for preparedness. As demonstrated in the preceding parables in this gospel, Matthew's arrangement shows the progressive transformation of our imperfect world into a world in which God truly reigns. In this respect, the fact that the parable commences in 25:1 with "then" in the future tense does not necessarily mean that it illustrates the reality of the end-time, but rather that it is the writer's way of speaking of a world in the progress of becoming like the coming kingdom of God, a reality that for the New Testament community had already begun. If the point of the parable is moral—the importance of sharing and being thoughtful—then that assumption seems to be invalidated by the conclusion of this and surrounding parables such as that of the Faithful Steward (24:45–51) and of the Talents (25:14–30), which portray God as an unmerciful and unsharing master.

At some point the light begins to dawn that Jesus is teaching at a whole different level here, for the metaphors don't comply. These hard teachings are not about outer actions or greater effort but about inner transformation, and they make most sense within this frame of reference. The reason the five bridesmaids who have oil don't and can't give it to the five who request it is that the oil symbolizes something that has to be individually created in you through your own spiritual maturing process. No one can give you your spiritual consciousness, and nobody can take it away from you. The oil stands for the quality of one's transformed consciousness, and it cannot be donated or shared with someone else. If we can consider the five wise bridesmaids as those who have acquired the "oil" of nondual consciousness, they can't possibly share it with others even if they wanted to; the others would not be ready yet to receive it.

In light of this summons to the personal transformation of consciousness, other difficult teachings in the gospels also begin to make sense. For instance, when speaking to his followers about the cost of discipleship, Jesus declares, "Do not think that I have come to bring peace to the earth; I have not come to bring peace, but a sword" (Matt 10:34). The parallel passage in Luke 12:51 speaks of bringing "division" rather than a sword. In either case, one's spiritual consciousness has both temporal and eternal consequences, and growth and transformation, though inner, are powerful and have both internal and external disruptive consequences. In Luke 14:25–26, when large crowds were traveling with Jesus, he turned and said to them, "Whoever comes to me and does not hate father and mother, wife and children, brothers and sisters, yes, and even life itself, cannot be my disciple. Whoever does not carry the cross and follow me cannot be my disciple." As we saw in chapter 6, statements such as these can be dismissed as Middle Eastern hyperbole. However, to do so is to miss their inner radicality, that there is a cost not only to Christian discipleship, but even more to inner spiritual growth and transformation.

Living Water

In Luke's gospel, Jesus' hard teaching on division within oneself and one's household is followed by a statement regarding the cost of discipleship and spiritual vulnerability: "For which of you, intending to build a tower, does not sit down first and estimate the cost, to see whether he has enough to complete it? Otherwise, when he has laid a foundation and is not able to finish, all who see it will begin to ridicule him, saying, 'This fellow began to build and was not able to finish.'" (Luke 14:28–29). This teaching seems to say that it's not enough simply to trust in God and throw caution to the winds; perhaps this is the meaning of the enigmatic statement in Matthew 10:16, where Jesus tells his disciples that both in the internal and external world, spirituality entails being "wise as serpents and innocent as doves."

In another difficult teaching a prospective follower asks Jesus, "First may I go home and bury my father?" Jesus' blunt response is, "let the dead bury their own dead" (Luke 9:59). If we are attached to our identity in this world—if that is the level our spiritual consciousness is operating on—we won't be able to pick up on the deeper teaching he is imparting, and we certainly won't be able to follow his lead.

These hard teachings are admittedly disorienting. We simply can't translate them into a sentimental theology that says, "Jesus wants you to be nice, to share, to try harder." Like his parables, Jesus' hard teachings are classic wisdom teachings that speak to the need for deepening our level of consciousness before we can emerge as complete human beings. Whatever we must say about Jesus' enigmatic teachings, they are designed to catch our attention and make us realize that there might be more to this iceberg called scripture than meets the eye.

In the parable of the Sheep and the Goats (Matt 25:31–46), God's judgment separates righteous individuals from unrighteous ones, that is, those trapped in egoic consciousness (their False Self) from those released into unitive consciousness (their True Self). Those lost to salvation are spiritually opposite of the righteous and blessed (25:32–33). The latter, acknowledged as righteous (not through effort but by virtue of affirming the preexistent gift of the True Self within), Jesus calls to himself, confirming that they are now prepared to inherit the kingdom that was prepared for them from the foundation of the world (see Matt 13:35). The reason for this favorable judgment is that by virtue of their unitive consciousness, the sheep lived and treated others (particularly the deprived and needy) as extensions of themselves, and consequently, as extensions of Christ.

Those gathered on Christ's left side, however, stigmatized as accursed, are still lost in the darkness of their egoic consciousness and not yet ready for the kingdom (eternal life; see 25:46). Their inability to meet the demands of the gospel is not the result of malice or bad intent, but the actual failure to see Christ in others. This then becomes the actual point of the discourse. In order to live according to the gospel of Christ and thus fulfill the entire law of God, one has to be able to see Christ in those who are marginalized. This, however, is a new and truly novel way of seeing, utterly dependent upon God's grace. Blessed are those who have received the gift of unitive consciousness, for they truly see and hear (see Matt 13:16). While it is easily to fault outsiders as morally impaired, what we see in this parable is that many are lost to salvation not as the result of evil deeds, but because of a certain kind of blindness that deprived their faith of actions directed to work and collaborate in the transformation of this world into the kingdom of God (see Luke 6:20–31). They will indeed listen, but never understand, and indeed look, but never perceive (Matt 13:14).

Revisiting the parable of the Faithful Steward (Matt 24:45–51), we understand now that the faithful servant, by virtue of unitive consciousness, indeed saw Christ in the members of his household, while the wicked servant, by virtue of egoic consciousness, only saw and sought his own pleasure. To summarize the parables in Matthew 24 and 25, we see that our world is tightly intertwined with traces of an ideal world, a world imagined as kingdom of God. Readers and listeners have a twofold task. First, to distinguish and separate these two ways of living, thinking, and being and thereby not falling victim to the mistake of identifying the egoic consciousness of this world with the unitive consciousness willed by God. In a second step, readers are asked to discern in what way Christ himself appears in this world in the form of fellow human beings who are in need of help that only they (we) can grant.

Reading the parables and other hard teachings of Jesus in timeless yet at the same time in situationally relevant ways allows biblical teachings to become personal narratives in which readers alike are confronted with the meaning of life flowing from faith in Christ. Those who do so are called "scribes trained for the kingdom of heaven" (a reference to the trained members of the Matthean community and to all those since privileged to see with unitive eyes and hear with unitive ears) and are like householders who bring from scripture what is new and what is old (see Matt 13:52).

Living Water

A Test Case for Interpreting Scripture with Different Levels of Consciousness

Perhaps the greatest mystery in spirituality is the nature of God, a mystery deeply embedded in the Christian scripture as well. Equally perplexing and ambiguous is the nature of our relationship with deity. Biblical talk about God is paradoxical. In passages such as Genesis 1:26–27, human beings are said to be made in the image of God, allowing for the kind of intimacy and fellowship between Adam, Eve, and God that we find narrated in Genesis 3:8, an intimacy shrouded in presence and hiddenness.

In ancient Judaism, angels were widely understood to be superhuman messengers of God, standing between God and humans and mediating God's will on earth. In the Hebrew Bible it is striking that various angels sometimes appear on earth in human guise. This includes a figure known as "the Angel of the Lord," who is regarded as the chief angel. In some passages he is identified as God, while in others he appears as a human. An example appears in Genesis 16, where the Lord speaks to Hagar, servant of Sarah, who has been exiled to the wilderness, pregnant with Abraham's child. The Angel of the Lord appears to her and tells her to return to her mistress. The author then surprises us by indicating that the angel is none other than Yahweh, the Lord. Hagar, of course, is astonished that she had "seen God and remained alive after seeing him" (Gen 16:13).

A similar ambiguity occurs in Genesis 18, this time with Abraham. In 18:1 we are told that "the Lord" appeared to Abraham, but when the episode is narrated, we learn that "three men" come to him. One of these three is later identified explicitly as "the Lord" (Gen 18:13). Such ambiguity continues in the famous episode of Moses and the burning bush in Exodus 3. In 3:2 we are told that the Angel of the Lord appears to Moses, yet later we are told it is "God" who calls to him out of the bush. There are numerous other texts that describe angels as God and, equally important, as human.

To the contrary, in Exodus 33:20 we read the well-known statement said to be uttered to Moses by God, "You cannot see my face; for no one shall see me and live" (see also John 1:18; 1 Timothy 6:16; 1 John 4:12). Nevertheless, each of these passages contain exceptions. For example, Exodus 33:22–23 indicates that Moses will be allowed to see God's back, but not God's face; in John 1:18, God is said to be fully with us in the incarnate Christ; and 1 John 4:12 tells believers that when they love other believers, God's love is perfected in them. In 2 Corinthians 3:7–18, Paul provides an explanation of Exodus 34:29–35, which speaks of Moses's encounter with God on Mount Sinai, an encounter that "made the skin of his face shine because he had been talking with God" (Exod 34:29).

Another passage that examines this conundrum is 1 Kings 19, a passage that records a memorable experience of the prophet Elijah on Mount Sinai. Elijah (his name means "Yahweh is my God"), persecuted by Jezebel (King Ahab's Phoenician wife) for his faithfulness to Yahweh, flees to Mount Sinai, where he prepares for an encounter with the divine: "Now there was a great wind, so strong that it was splitting mountains and breaking rocks in pieces before Yahweh, but Yahweh was not in the wind; and after the wind an earthquake, but Yahweh was not in the earthquake; and after the earthquake a fire, but Yahweh was not in the fire; and after the fire a sound of sheer silence" (1 Kgs 19:11–12; these last few words are traditionally translated "a still small voice").

Elijah's experience on Mount Sinai reminds us of the climactic experience of Moses with God at the same location, the vision of God in darkness described at Exodus 33:17–23. If even Moses is able to see only God's back, is there any hope that anyone else can see God's "face" and live? For practical purposes, the God of the Old Testament is a hidden God, hidden yet everywhere present. Yet, according to the prophet Isaiah, the God who is hidden can be known by the person who does not seek to "see" God, but rather to obey God's will: "I dwell in the high and holy place," says the Lord, "and also with those who are contrite and humble in spirit" (57:15).

Because God is a person who is alive and active and yet has an awesome, even overwhelming personality, friendship with God is both a privilege and yet elusive. While it is difficult to live with God, it is impossible to live without God. Yet the hiddenness of God—perhaps even God's absence—seems the dominant reality for many seekers throughout history.

Given the wide spectrum of descriptions in scripture of the nature of God and of the divine-human relationship, what are we to make of this vast and bewildering array of possibilities? Some call them paradoxical, others contradictory, but as we have been saying all along, there are various explanations. One possibility is situational and contextual, another is perspectival, and yet another is accommodationist, meaning that scripture is primarily narrative, and like great literature, readers are given as much as they understand. As many biblical exegetes and commentators have noted, the biblical text is polyvalent, meaning it contains numerous levels of meaning. Within the readers, however, are levels of perception, comprehension, and understanding.

What if we approach scripture, particularly its difficult passages, images, and even doctrines, through the lens of levels of consciousness? Might it be possible that people at different levels of spiritual awareness will see and hear different things? And might this be intentional by the author(s) of scripture as well? If we take Ken Wilber's modified list of levels of consciousness, some will see nothing of God and proclaim themselves atheists or agnostics, for they are unable to see God and live; some may be aware of a "still small voice" within, but nothing else; others, like Adam and Eve, may hear God speak and even sense God's presence; yet others may see something of God's presence and nature, but only that which can be described as God's back side. At a higher level of consciousness, a few may come to know God intuitively, even to the point of "seeing" God and "hearing" God's voice; and a select few will be able to say, like Jesus did, that "the Father and I are one" (John 10:30).

Ultimately, may an ever-increasing number of us experience what Jesus had in mind when he told his listeners, "Ask, and it will be given you; search, and you will find; knock, and the door will be opened for you" (Matt 7:7/Luke 11:9).

Questions for Discussion and Reflection

Having read chapter 12, answer the following questions, writing your answers in a journal. If you are in a group study, be prepared to share your answers with those in the group.

1. In your estimation, does one fulfill the commandment to love God and neighbor as oneself by doing or by being? Explain your answer.
2. In your estimation, does the claim, "the Father and I are one" belong only to Jesus Christ, or does it apply to other humans as well? If the latter, to whom might this affirmation apply?
3. After reading this chapter, what did you learn about the commandment to love your neighbor as yourself?
4. When reading the parable of the Good Samaritan, with whom do you identify, the victim or his rescuer? Explain your answer.

Hard Teachings of Jesus

5. When reading the parable of the Prodigal Son, with whom do you identify, the prodigal or the older son? Explain your answer.

6. After reading this chapter, what did you learn about Jesus' encounter with Nicodemus?

7. What is your answer to the famous Zen *koan*, "What is the sound of one hand clapping"?

8. After reading this chapter, what did you learn about being "born of water and Spirit" in John 3:5?

9. After reading this chapter, what did you learn about the parable of the Wise and Foolish Bridesmaids in Matthew 25:1–13?

10. What, for you, is the "hardest" teaching in scripture? Explain your answer.

11. After reading this chapter, what did you learn about the meaning of Jesus' declaration that discipleship entails hating loved ones and even life itself?

12. After reading this chapter, what did you learn about the meaning of the parable of the Sheep and the Goats in Matthew 25:31–46?

13. After reading this chapter, what did you learn about the nature of God and about the divine-human relationship?

14. After reading this chapter or book, what did you learn about interpreting scripture with different levels of consciousness?

Epilogue

PART OF THE PARADOX of the parables is that hardly any of them are "religious" in the direct sense of the word. It is apparent that in approaching the common people Jesus was able to talk of the concerns of God in everyday terms. In his novel *Doctor Zhivago*, Boris Pasternak remarks on this when he has his hero say: "It has always been assumed that the most important things in the Gospels are the ethical maxims and commandments. But for me the most important thing is that Christ speaks in parables taken from life, that He explains the truth in terms of everyday reality."[1]

Parables inform, but their primary purpose is to elicit a response. The response will be to move positively toward Jesus and his message or negatively away from him and his concerns. In seeking a response, parables appeal to the emotions. The description of the extravagant love and grace of God and the threat of judgment, the antitheses of wisdom and foolishness, and the common features of everyday life and relations are framed to urge people to understand that God's kingdom is already at work and to persuade them to decide to be involved in that kingdom. However, it is not enough to study the parables, admire them, and reflect on them; the response parables require is action.

Like much of scripture, parables are primarily concerned with identity couched in mindset and levels of consciousness, for the present kingdom of God entails decision about one's nature, identity, and allegiance. Identities formed by the parables lead to people who understand grace and its demands and take them seriously enough to respond, who know the joy of the kingdom and are willing to celebrate, who are transformed and enabled to perceive and not just to see, to love their neighbors and take care of

---

1. Pasternak, *Doctor Zhivago*, 40.

Epilogue

the poor and troubled, who are wise and faithful in view of God's ongoing defeat of evil.

In addition, parables give us the language with which to think and theologize. They open imagistic worlds that compel allegiance, challenge belief and action, and transform the way we see and think. For these reasons, they deserve all the attention we can give them.

I end our study of the parables and a parabolic approach to scripture with a prayer for openness to renewed consciousness by theologian Howard Thurman (1900–1981), guide and spiritual mentor to generations of believers.

> The old song of my spirit has wearied itself out. It has long ago been learned by heart so that now it repeats itself over and over, bringing no added joy to my days or lift to my spirit. It is a good song, measured to a rhythm to which I am bound by ties of habit and timidity of mind. The words belong to old experiences which once sprang fresh as water from a mountain crevice fed by melting snows. But my life has passed beyond to other levels where the old song is meaningless. I demand of the old song that it meet the need of present urgencies. Also, I know that the work of the old song, perfect in its place, is not for the new demand!
>
> I will sing a new song. As difficult as it is, I must learn the new song that is capable of meeting the new need. I must fashion new worlds born of all the new growth of my life, my mind, and my spirit. I must prepare for new melodies that have never been mine before, that all that is within me may lift my voice unto God. How I love the old familiarity of the wearied melody—how I shrink from the harsh discords of the new untried harmonies.
>
> Teach me, my Father, that I might learn with the abandonment and enthusiasm of Jesus, the fresh new accent, the untried melody, to meet the need of the untried morrow. Thus, I may rejoice with each new day and delight my spirit in each fresh unfolding.
>
> I will sing, this day, a new song unto Thee, O God.[2]

---

2. Thurman, *Meditations of the Heart*, 206–7.

Bibliography

Albright, W. F., and C. S. Mann. *Matthew*. The Anchor Bible 26. Garden City, NY: Doubleday, 1971.
Allison, Dale C., Jr. *Constructing Jesus*. Grand Rapids: Baker, 2010.
———. *The Historical Christ and the Theological Jesus*. Grand Rapids: Eerdmans, 2009.
———. *Jesus of Nazareth: Millenarian Prophet*. Minneapolis: Fortress, 1998.
Anderson, Bernhard W. *Contours of Old Testament Theology*. Minneapolis: Fortress, 1999.
Bailey, Kenneth Ewing. *Poet and Peasant: A Literary Cultural Approach to the Parables in Luke*. Grand Rapids: Eerdmans, 1976.
Barclay, William. *And Jesus Said: A Handbook on the Parables of Jesus*. Philadelphia: Westminster, 1970.
Barnhart, Bruno. *Second Simplicity: The Inner Shape of Christianity*. Mahwah, NJ: Paulist, 1999.
Bourgeault, Cynthia. *The Wisdom Jesus: Transforming Heart and Mind–a New Perspective on Christ and His Message*. Boston: Shambhala, 2008.
Borg, Marcus J. *The God We Never Knew*. San Francisco: HarperSanFrancisco, 1998.
———. *The Heart of Christianity*. San Francisco: HarperSanFrancisco, 2004.
———. *Meeting Jesus Again for the First Time*. San Francisco: HarperSanFrancisco, 1994.
———. *Reading the Bible Again for the First Time*. San Francisco: HarperSanFrancisco, 2001.
———. *Speaking Christian*. New York: HarperOne, 2011.
———, and N. T. Wright. *The Meaning of Jesus: Two Visions*. San Francisco: HarperSanFrancisco, 1999.
Bowker, John. "Mystery and Parable: Mark 4:1–20." *Journal of Theological Studies* 25 (1974) 300–317.
———, et al. *The New Jerome Biblical Commentary*. Upper Saddle River, NJ: Prentice Hall, 1990.
Bruner, Frederick Dale. *Matthew: A Commentary*. 2 vols. Grand Rapids: Eerdmans, 1990.
Cox, Harvey. *When Jesus Came to Harvard: Making Moral Choices Today*. Boston: Houghton Mifflin, 2004.
Craddock, Fred B. *Luke*. Interpretation: A Bible Commentary for Teaching and Preaching. Louisville: John Knox, 1990.
Crossan, John Dominic. *In Parables: The Challenge of the Historical Jesus*. New York: Harper & Row, 1973.
Cullmann, Oscar. *Christ and Time*. Philadelphia: Westminster, 1950.
Culpepper. R. Alan. "The Gospel of Luke." In *The New Interpreter's Bible* 9:3–490.

Bibliography

Danker, Frederick W. *Jesus and the New Age: A Commentary on St. Luke's Gospel*. Rev. ed. Philadelphia: Fortress, 1988.

Davies, W. D., and Dale C. Allison. *A Critical and Exegetical Commentary on the Gospel According to Matthew*. 3 vols. International Critical Commentary. Edinburgh: T&T Clark, 1988–1997.

Dodd, C. H. *The Parables of the Kingdom*. London: Collins, 1961.

Fitzmyer, Joseph A. *The Gospel According to Luke*. 2 vols. The Anchor Bible: 28, 28A. Garden City, NY: Doubleday, 1981, 1985.

Fowler, James W. *Stages of Faith*. New York: Harper & Row, 1981.

Fox, Matthew. *Creation Spirituality*. San Francisco: HarperSanFrancisco, 1991.

———. *Original Blessing*. Santa Fe, NM: Bear & Co., 1983.

Hargreaves, John. *A Guide to the Parables*. Valley Forge, PA: Judson, 1975.

Jeremias, Joachim. *The Parables of Jesus*. Rev. ed. Translated by S. H. Hooke. New York: Scribner's Sons, 1963.

Kelsey, Morton T. *Afterlife: The Other Side of Dying*. New York: Crossroad, 2005.

Locker, Markus. *The New World of Jesus' Parables*. Newcastle upon Tyne, UK: Cambridge Scholars Publishing, 2008.

Manson, T. W. *The Teaching of Jesus*. 2nd ed. Cambridge: Cambridge University Press, 1935.

Marion, Jim. *Putting on the Mind of Christ*. Charlottesville, VA: Hampton Roads, 2000.

McGrath, Alister E. *Christian Theology: An Introduction*. 5th ed. Malden, MA: Wiley-Blackwell, 2011.

McLaren, Brian D. *A New Kind of Christian: A Tale of Two Friends on a Spiritual Journey*. San Francisco: Jossey-Bass, 2001.

———. *A New Kind of Christianity: Ten Questions That Are Transforming the Faith*. New York: HarperCollins, 2010.

———. *The Secret Message of Jesus: Uncovering the Truth That Could Change Everything*. Nashville: W Publishing, 2006.

Meier, John P. *A Marginal Jew: Probing the Authenticity of the Parables*. New Haven, CT: Yale University Press, 2016.

Mohler Jr., R. Albert. *Tell Me the Stories of Jesus: The Explosive Power of Jesus' Parables*. Nashville: Thomas Nelson, 2022.

Pasternak, Boris. *Doctor Zhivago*. New York: New American Library, 1972.

Rohr, Richard. *Falling Upward: A Spirituality for the Two Halves of Life*. San Francisco: Jossey-Bass, 2011.

———. *The Good News According to Luke*. New York: Crossroad, 1997.

———. *Immortal Diamond: The Search for Our True Self*. San Francisco: Jossey-Bass, 2013.

———. *The Naked Now: Learning to See as the Mystics See*. New York: Crossroad, 2009.

———. *The Universal Christ*. New York: Convergent, 2019.

———. *What the Mystics Know*. New York: Crossroad, 2015.

Sanders, E. P. *Jesus and Judaism*. Philadelphia: Fortress, 1985.

———. "Jesus: His Religious Type." *Reflections* 87 (1992) 4–12.

Scott, Bernard Brandon. *Hear Then the Parable*. Minneapolis: Fortress, 1989.

Shillington, V. George. *Jesus and His Parables: Interpreting the Parables of Jesus Today*. Edinburgh: T&T Clark, 1997.

Snodgrass, Klyne R. "Are the Parables Still the Bedrock of the Jesus Tradition?" *Journal for the Study of the Historical Jesus* 15 (2017) 131–46.

Bibliography

———. *Stories and Intent: A Comprehensive Guide to the Parables of Jesus*. Grand Rapids: Eerdmans, 2008.

Spong, John Shelby. *Eternal Life: A New Vision*. New York: HarperOne, 2009.

———. *Liberating the Gospels: Reading the Bible with Jewish Eyes*. San Francisco: HarperSanFrancisco, 1996.

———. *Rescuing the Bible from Fundamentalism*. San Francisco: HarperSanFrancisco, 1991.

———. *Why Christianity Must Change or Die: A Bishop Speaks to Believers in Exile*. New York: HarperOne, 1999.

Sviri, Sara, *The Taste of Hidden Things*. Inverness, CA: Golden Sufi Center, 1997.

Taylor, Barbara Brown. *The Seeds of Heaven: Sermons on the Gospel of Matthew*. Louisville: Westminster John Knox, 2004.

Thurman, Howard. *Meditations of the Heart*. Richmond, IN: Friends United, 1994.

———. *Sermons on the Parables*. Edited by David B. Gowler and Kipton E. Jensen. Maryknoll, NY: Orbis, 2018.

Vande Kappelle, Robert P. *Beyond Belief: Faith, Science, and the Value of Unknowing*. Eugene, OR: Wipf & Stock, 2012.

———. *Dark Splendor: Spiritual Fitness for the Second Half of Life*. Eugene, OR: Wipf & Stock, 2015.

———. *Holistic Happiness: Spirituality and a Healing Lifestyle*. Eugene, OR: Wipf $ Stock, 2022.

———. *In the Potter's Workshop: Experiencing the Divine Presence in Everyday Life*. Eugene, OR: Wipf & Stock, 2019.

———. *Power Revealed: The Message of Luke–Acts—Then and Now*. Eugene, OR: Wipf & Stock, 2019.

———. *The Scandal of Divine Love*. Eugene, OR: Wipf & Stock, 2017.

———. *Securing Life: The Enduring Message of the Bible*. Eugene, OR: Wipf & Stock, 2016.

———. *Truth Revealed: The Message of the Gospel of John—Then and Now*. Eugene, OR: Wipf & Stock, 2014.

———. *Understanding Scripture: Forty Things to Know about the Christian Bible*. Eugene, OR: Wipf & Stock, 2020.

———. *Walking on Water: Living into a New Way of Thinking*. Eugene, OR: Wipf & Stock, 2020.

Via, Dan Otto. *The Parables: Their Literary and Existential Dimension*. Philadelphia: Fortress, 1967.

Wierzbieka, Anna. *What Did Jesus Mean? Explaining the Sermon on the Mount and the Parables in Simple and Universal Human Concepts*. Oxford: Oxford University Press, 2001.

Witherington, Ben. *Jesus the Sage: The Pilgrimage of Wisdom*. Minneapolis: Fortress, 1994.

Zimmerman, Ruben. "Memory and Jesus' Parables: J. P. Meier's Explosion and the Restoration of the 'Bedrock' of Jesus' Speech." *Journal for the Study of the Historical Jesus* 16 (2018) 156–72.

Index

Abraham, 7, 160
Allison, Dale, 91
Angel of the Lord, 160
Anselm of Canterbury, 6
apocalyptic(ism), 73–74, 81, 88–89, 94, 106, 107–9
Apostles' Creed, 9
atonement theology, 6
Augustine, 25, 116

Barnhart, Bruno, 11
Basil of Caesarea, 50
beatitudes, 45, 63, 111–17
Blake, William, 42
Bonhoeffer, Dietrich, 85
Borg, Marcus, 9, 55, 91
Bowker, John, 119, 120
Browning, Elizabeth Barrett, 81
Buddha, the, 40, 44

Chesterton, G. K., 46
Chopra, Deepak, 14
christology, 24
Cloud of Unknowing, 16
consciousness, levels of, 27–36, 139, 140–41, 147, 158, 160–62, 165
    shift (change) in, 4, 46, 47, 48, 58, 59, 66, 82, 102, 121, 133, 135, 138, 140, 141, 149, 151, 157, 166
conversion (second birth), 32, 35, 42, 43, 154–56
Crossan, John Dominic, 152
Cullmann, Oscar, 109

D'Arcy, Paula, 21
death and resurrection of the Self, 38–42
discipleship, 85, 115, 125, 129, 145, 157
Dodd, C. H., 3, 78
dualist consciousness. *See* egoic consciousness

ego. *See* False Self
egoic consciousness, 3–4, 24, 27, 28–29, 30–33, 38, 41, 43, 44, 45, 47, 53, 79, 80, 89, 133, 136, 138, 141, 148, 153, 158, 159
Elijah, 161
Eliot, T. S., 18
eschatology, 73, 88–100, 106, 156
    definition of, 77
    realized, 74, 77–83, 84
eschaton, 77, 107

False Self, 15, 22, 36, 38–40, 44, 66, 142, 144, 148, 158
first half of life, 3, 4, 20, 21, 22, 29–33, 46, 121, 137–38, 148
    spirituality, 18, 29
    tasks of, 15–16
five halves of life, 29–36
Fox, Matthew, 14
Francis of Assisi, 41

Gandhi, Mohandas, 9, 46
God, 35
    as Father, 62, 70
    hiddenness of, 161
    image of, 160

Index

God (*cont.*)
   knowing, 161
   love of, 23, 25, 50, 62, 83, 126
   nature of, 160, 161
   seeing and hearing, 160–62
   as Sower, 136
Golden Rule, 71
good and evil, 27, 32, 80
gospel
   and genre, 5
Gregory of Nazianzus, 50
Gregory of Nyssa, 50

Hargreaves, John, 1
heaven, 22, 41, 43, 80–81, 84–85, 90, 106, 110–11, 116
hell, 22, 23, 80, 116
Holy Bible, 4, 52–59, 162
   authority of, 53
   genre in, 4–6
   as great literature, 57
   and levels of consciousness, 162
   parabolic approach to, 6, 10, 28, 57–59
   polyvalency of, 53, 161
   reading and studying, 4, 28, 33, 52–55, 59
   as sacred, 55, 56, 57
   as Word of God, 4
Holy Spirit, 13, 35, 40, 46, 77, 78, 82, 83, 84, 102, 109, 115, 155, 156
Hugh of St. Victor, 42

interabiding, 47, 151–52

Jabay, Earl, 22
Jeremias, Joachim, 3
Jesus Christ, 45, 47
   as apocalyptic prophet, 91, 95–100
   death of, 6, 9, 22, 102
   as divine, 24
   hard teachings of, 151–59
   having the "mind" of, 47–50, 120
   humanity of, 24
   incarnation of, 24
   and kingdom of God, 74–83, 88–92, 125–26, 134
   life of, 10, 103
   motto of, 49
   as nondual sage, 28, 46
   as prophetic sage, 60–71
   resurrection of, 56–57, 102–7, 109
   Second Coming of, 83–86, 109, 130
   as Son of Man, 24, 96, 97, 106–7
   as storyteller, 2, 58
   as teacher, 61–71, 133
   use of hyperbole, 63–64, 125, 157
   use of parables, 119–49
   and wealth, 49, 98, 99, 124–25, 128–30
   See also christology
John, gospel of, 2, 10–11, 22, 23, 24, 28, 39, 46, 47, 62, 79–80, 84, 85, 96, 104, 105
Jones, G. V., 3
Julian of Norwich, 18
Jülicher, Adolf, 66
Jung, Carl, 38, 41, 112

Keating, Thomas, 152
Kelsey, Morton, 110–11
Kierkegaard, Søren, 17, 114
kingdom of God, 22, 25, 59, 73–83, 88–92, 107, 114, 116, 117, 123–24, 126, 134, 138–40, 141, 142, 143, 145, 147, 148, 155, 156, 158, 159, 165
   definition of, 75, 78–79, 138, 146
   as "eternal life," 2, 80, 83, 111, 117, 159
   mystery (secret of), 43, 44, 108, 121, 125, 139
   nature of, 75, 138, 139
   in the Sermon on the Mount, 110–17
   as a state of consciousness, 151

living water, 10–12, 46, 121
Lord's Prayer, 78, 93, 114, 126
lostness, 126, 142, 144
love, 18–19, 20, 22, 29, 35, 46, 85–86, 116, 126, 138, 145, 152
   of neighbor, 152
Luke, gospel of, 42, 96, 104, 105, 122, 123–30
   and table-fellowship, 128
   and wealth and possessions, 128–30

Marion, Jim, 151

Index

Mark, gospel of, 14, 69, 75, 78, 97, 104, 119–20, 121, 129, 130
mashal, meshalim, 58, 64, 65, 67, 122, 152–53
Matthew, gospel of, 42, 69–71, 104, 108, 111–17, 130, 133–49
    setting of, 69, 134, 159
McGrath, Alistair, 8
McLaren, Brian, 22, 54, 75n1
Meier, John P., 119n1
Merton, Thomas, 39
metanoia, 141, 147
Moses, 7, 42, 70, 160, 161

Nicodemus, 62, 94, 154–55
nondual (unitive) consciousness, 3–4, 11, 25, 27–28, 29, 34, 40, 43, 44, 46, 47, 48, 50, 136, 138, 139, 140, 142, 146, 148, 151, 153, 157, 158, 159

original sin, 6

Panikkar, Raimon, 50
parable of
    the Dishonest Steward, 129
    the Dragnet, 134, 135, 136, 140
    the Faithful Steward, 157, 159
    the Good Samaritan, 66, 93, 121, 122–23, 153
    the Hidden Treasure, 134, 139
    the Laborers in the Vineyard, 45, 49, 153
    the Lost Coin, 126, 127
    the Lost Sheep, 127, 141, 142–44
    the Mustard Seed, 79, 126, 134, 139
    the Pharisee and the Tax Collector, 129
    the Pounds, 130
    the Precious Pearl, 98, 134, 139–40
    the Prodigal Son, 121, 126, 127, 138, 142, 146, 153
    the Rich Fool, 124
    the Rich Man and Lazarus, 129
    the Sheep and the Goats, 96, 141, 145, 148, 158
    the Sower, 119, 134, 135–37, 138, 141, 143
    the Talents, 66, 141, 145, 146, 157
    the Two Sons, 141, 143, 144, 146–47
    the Unforgiving Servant, 49, 141, 145–46
    the Unjust Judge, 129
    the Vineyard, 147
    the Wedding Banquet, 141, 147, 148–49
    the Wheat and the Weeds, 134, 135, 136, 137–38, 139, 140
    the Wise and Foolish Bridesmaids, 156–57
    the Yeast, 122, 126, 134, 139
parables, 1, 2, 58, 64, 144, 165–66
    aesthetic nature of, 3
    and allegory, 3, 66, 133, 134, 145, 148
    definition of, 66
    eschatological nature of, 66, 122, 123, 135
    as example stories, 1, 122, 124
    as extended narratives, 1, 65, 67
    function of, 66, 120, 165–66
    of Jesus, 1, 2, 10, 65–66, 119–49
    and the kingdom of God, 44, 93, 121, 122, 124, 126, 134, 135, 138–40, 141, 142, 143, 145, 147, 148
    as "moments of truth," 2
    and nondual consciousness, 3–4
    as sacred wisdom, 58
    and transformative change, 1, 135, 140, 141
    and wisdom, 2–3, 67
Pasternak, Boris, 165
Paul (apostle), 2, 9, 34, 43, 47, 49, 53, 65, 76, 77, 82, 84, 97, 103, 104, 105, 106, 108, 113, 117, 125, 128, 151, 160
perichoresis, 50, 151
pre-understanding, 4
proverb(s), 5, 57, 58, 63, 64, 65, 67, 152

Rahner, Karl, 48
Revelation, book of, 4–5, 80, 84, 85, 109
Richard of St. Victor, 42–43
Ricoeur, Paul, 17
Rohr, Richard, 40, 41, 50
Rumi, Jallaludin, 48

Index

salvation, 22, 73, 159
    definition of, 7
    doctrine of, 6–10, 23
Sanders, E. P., 90
Schweitzer, Albert, 95
Scott, Bernard Brandon, 152
scripture. *See* Holy Bible
second half of life, 30–36, 140, 148, 153
    qualities of, 16, 17, 19–20
    spirituality, 13–25, 30
    tasks of, 21
seeing rightly, 28, 42–44, 57, 133, 146, 152, 159
Sermon on the Mount/Plain, 69, 70, 98, 110, 111–17, 123, 133, 147
sin
    doctrine of, 23
Snodgrass, Klyne, 144
soul, 15, 16, 18, 28, 36
spirituality, 42, 53, 148, 158
    definition of, 13–14
    kenotic, 47–50
    role of, 38, 40
    stages of, 15
    and theological unlearning, 21–25

Taylor, Barbara Brown, 135
Teresa of Ávila, 18
Thurman, Howard, 166
True Self, 22, 36, 38–40, 43, 44, 66, 137, 138, 139, 140, 142, 144, 148

unitive consciousness. *See* nondual consciousness

Via, Dan, 3
vine and branches, 28, 47, 152

Wilber, Ken, 17, 27, 162
Williams, Charles, 114
wisdom literature, 64–65, 68
Witherington, Ben, 64

Yates, William Butler, 38

www.ingramcontent.com/pod-product-compliance
Lightning Source LLC
Chambersburg PA
CBHW050809160426
43192CB00010B/1703